Yemen

Yemen

BY LIZ SONNEBORN

Enchantment of the World™
Second Series

CHILDREN'S PRESS®

An Imprint of Scholastic Inc.

Frontispiece: **Bab al-Yaman gate, Sanaa**

Consultant: Stephen Caton, Professor of Contemporary Arab Studies, Department of
Anthropology, Harvard University, Cambridge, Massachusetts
Please note: All statistics are as up-to-date as possible at the time of publication.

Book production by The Design Lab

Library of Congress Cataloging-in-Publication Data
Sonneborn, Liz.
 Yemen / by Liz Sonneborn.
    pages cm — (Enchantment of the world)
 Includes bibliographical references and index.
 ISBN 978-0-531-23299-6 (library binding)
 1. Yemen (Republic)—Juvenile literature. I. Title.
 DS247.Y48S652 2015
 953.3—dc23   2015021147

1 2 3 4 5 6 7 8 9 10 R 25 24 23 22 21 20 19 18 17 16

Boy at a cattle fair

Contents

CHAPTER 1   The Iron Lady **8**

CHAPTER 2   Mountains and Deserts **18**

CHAPTER 3   Wild Things **30**

CHAPTER 4   Country in Conflict **42**

CHAPTER 5   Governing Yemen **64**

CHAPTER 6	A Struggling Economy	74
CHAPTER 7	The People of Yemen	84
CHAPTER 8	A Muslim Country	92
CHAPTER 9	A Culture of Old and New	102
CHAPTER 10	Yemeni Ways	112
	Timeline	128
	Fast Facts	130
	To Find Out More	134
	Index	136

Left to right: **Farmer, children, market, camel jumping, schoolchildren**

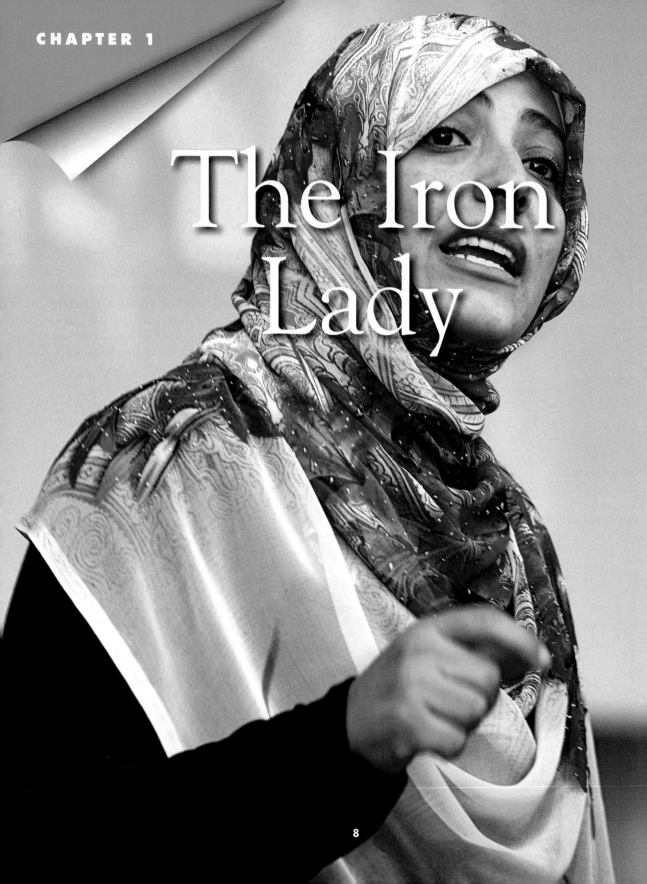

CHAPTER 1

The Iron Lady

ONE NIGHT IN FEBRUARY 2011, A YOUNG WOMAN named Tawakkol Karman emerged from the crowd gathered at Tahrir Square in Sanaa. The city was the capital of Yemen, a Middle Eastern country at the southern tip of the Arabian Peninsula.

Karman was not wearing a *niqab*, a loose black garment commonly worn by Yemeni women when they appear in public. A niqab covers a woman from head to toe, except for a small slit that reveals her eyes. Karman instead wore a black gown with a floral headscarf that left her face uncovered. Many men and women in Yemen considered her style of dress immodest. But Karman had decided it was necessary for her chosen role—that of a political activist. Several years before, during a televised conference, she pointedly removed her veil. "I thought before I spoke my mind, I should show you my face," she told the television audience. "A woman who wants to play an influential role must not create a barrier between herself and others."

Opposite: **Before becoming a political activist, Tawakkol Karman was a journalist. She was known in Yemen for fighting for freedom of the press.**

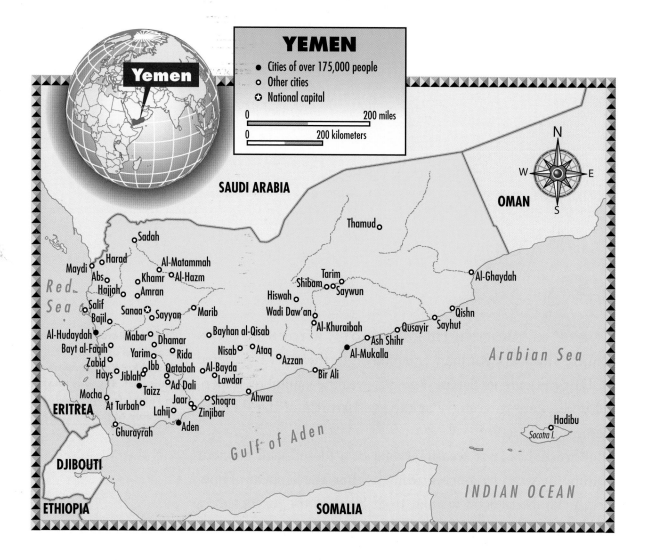

YEMEN

- Cities of over 175,000 people
- Other cities
- National capital

0 — 200 miles
0 — 200 kilometers

SAUDI ARABIA

OMAN

Thamud

Sadah

Maydi   Harad
Abs   Al-Matammah
Hajjah   Khamr   Al-Hazm
Amran   Tarim
Red   Salif   Shibam   Saywun
Sea   Bajil   Sanaa   Sayyan   Marib   Hiswah
           Mabar   Dhamar   Wadi Daw'an   Qishn
Al-Hudaydah   Yarim   Rida   Bayhan al-Qisab   Al-Khuraibah   Qusayir   Sayhut
Bayt al-Faqih   Nisab   Ataq   Ash Shir
Zabid   Ibb   Qatabah   Azzan   Al-Mukalla
Hays   Jiblah   Al-Bayda   Bir Ali
       Ad Dali   Lawdar
Mocha   Taizz   Jaar   Shoqra   Ahwar
       At Turbah   Lahij   Zinjibar
ERITREA   Ghurayrah   Aden

Al-Ghaydah

Arabian Sea

Hadibu
Socotra I.

Gulf of Aden

DJIBOUTI

INDIAN OCEAN

ETHIOPIA   SOMALIA

In Tahrir Square, Karman stepped on top of an overturned crate and addressed the crowd in a similarly forthright manner. She decried the "combination of a dictatorship, corruption, poverty, and unemployment" that was destroying hope among the Yemenis, especially the nation's youth. "Injustice and corruption are exploding while opportunities for a good life are coming to an end," she declared. The crowd, filled mostly with young male students, answered by chanting, "Saleh's days are numbered!"

Fighting the System

Ali Abdullah Saleh had risen to power in 1978, the year before Tawakkol Karman was born. He was then the president of the Yemen Arab Republic (YAR), the country in which Karman had grown up. In 1990, Saleh became the president of the Republic of Yemen, which was created when the YAR and the People's Republic of Yemen united to become one nation. In the decades since, Saleh had proved to be a ruthless ruler, funneling money and jobs to his relatives and associates, while most Yemenis lived in desperate poverty.

Yemen has one of the highest poverty rates of any country in the Arab world. More than half its population is living in poverty.

In college, Karman began studying the politics of Yemen. She decided to work to change the system. Karman was particularly concerned with how journalists were treated in Yemen. When journalists wrote something the Saleh regime did not like, they were often sent to jail on false charges.

After graduating, Karman married and had three children. But she also continued to be an activist. In 2005, she founded Women Journalists Without Chains, an organization dedicated to promoting freedom of speech and women's rights. She tried

Protesters sit in the tent city in Tahrir Square in 2011. Yemenis put up more than three thousand tents during the protests.

to establish a service that provided Yemenis with news reports by way of text messages on their phones. The government, however, shut the service down. Karman also became a prominent member of Islah, a conservative religious party opposed to Saleh.

Protests at Change Square

Karman's work as an activist and a politician left her frustrated. Yemenis had been protesting against the Saleh regime since 2004, yet she did not see the lives of average Yemenis getting any better. But protests against dictatorial regimes in other parts of the Arab world were starting to have effects. In the African country of Tunisia, dictator Zine El Abidine Ben Ali was unable to maintain power in the face of mass protests, and he fled the country on January 14, 2011.

In Yemen, the demonstrations against Saleh grew. Using Facebook and Twitter, Karman and others invited friends to join a protest at Tahrir Square. Gathering around a statue titled *The Wisdom of the Yemeni People*, they cheered the Tunisian revolution and called for Saleh to resign. Word spread, and more and more people came out. Within a week, hundreds of people were joining the daily protests. In a month and a half, the number had grown to ten thousand. The protesters built a tent city in Tahrir Square, which they renamed Change Square. Eventually, the tent city grew to have a population of one hundred thousand. It had its own hospital, dining hall, movie theater, and mosque (an Islamic house of worship). The protests spread to Taizz, Aden, and other Yemeni cities.

At first, Saleh dismissed the protesters in Yemen as small in number and unreasonable. He tried to calm them by promising jobs to recent college graduates. He then tried to shame them by denouncing the mixing of male and female protesters as an insult to Islam. He finally tried to terrorize the protesters by sending in security forces to beat and even kill people who were speaking out against him. On March 18, snipers above the square fired on the protesters below. At least fifty-two people were killed and two hundred were wounded. Instead of being scared away, the protesters continued the fight.

A Prize for Peace

In October, while at the camp in Change Square, Karman learned that she had received the Nobel Peace Prize for her role in the protests. (She shared the award with two activists from Liberia, Ellen Johnson Sirleaf and Leymah Gbowee.) Nicknamed the Iron Lady in Yemen because of her determination, Karman, at thirty-two years old, was then the youngest person ever to be given the prestigious honor. She was also the second Muslim (a practitioner of Islam) to win the prize. As word spread about the award, cheers erupted throughout Change Square. Just a month later, the protesters received even better news. Saleh had resigned as president of Yemen.

At the Nobel awards ceremony, Karman predicted "the birth of a new world" in Yemen and other Arab nations, in which all people would have "freedom, democracy, and dignity." She stated that the Nobel Prize was not just for her, but "a declaration and recognition of the whole world for the

triumph of the peaceful revolution of Yemen and as an appreciation of the sacrifices of its great peaceful people."

Tawakkol Karman receives the Nobel Peace Prize at a ceremony in 2011. One of the two other winners, Liberia's Leymah Gbowee, stands behind her.

War Breaks Out

The protesters had succeeded in removing Saleh, but Yemen's "peaceful revolution" was not to remain peaceful for long. An early indication of the violence to come appeared the day of the inauguration of Saleh's successor, Abdu Rabbu Mansour Hadi. Just after he was sworn in as president, a bomb exploded outside a presidential compound and killed twenty-five people. The authorities suspected that al-Qaeda in the Arabian Peninsula was behind the attack. This powerful branch of al-Qaeda, a terrorist network, had formed in Yemen in 2009.

Houthi supporters march in the streets of Sanaa.

Al-Qaeda was not the only faction in Yemen eager to challenge Hadi's rule. Many Yemenis in the south were part of a movement that wanted the region to break away and form its own country. In the north, a group called the Houthis was hoping to take over Yemen and establish its own government. The Houthi group was led by descendants of the Prophet Muhammad, the founder of the religion of Islam. To many Yemenis, this gave them a religious legitimacy that the national government did not have. The Houthis had been part of the opposition to the Saleh regime. In particular, they opposed Saleh's corruption, making them tremendously popular. In Yemen's rural areas, many groups had long looked to local rulers called sheikhs for leadership rather than to officials in Sanaa. The sheikhs had shifting loyalties and were willing to back whatever group offered them the most money and support, including the Houthis.

In this powder keg, it was hardly surprising that Yemen's peaceful revolution evaporated. Long-simmering tensions exploded as the Houthis grew in strength and began using violence to force others to accept their will. In September 2014, the Houthis managed to take over the capital. A group of Houthi rebels broke into Tawakkol Karman's house in Sanaa while she was in the United States attending a human rights conference. They photographed themselves sitting on her bed holding rifles and downloaded the image to Facebook. During a television interview, a visibly shaken Karman declared, "The peaceful revolution has been betrayed, stabbed in the back by the Houthis." In the months to come, the country erupted into civil war, with multiple factions battling for supremacy. Adding to the chaos was the involvement of foreign governments, particularly Saudi Arabia, whose 2015 bombing campaign left large swaths of Yemen a smoldering ruin.

Such political violence and upheaval is hardly unique in the country's history. One of the oldest continually inhabited areas in the world, Yemen has often been in conflict with outsiders. But just as often, Yemenis have been at war with themselves. When they united to form the Republic of Yemen in 1990, the Yemeni people hoped that together they could all prosper. Unfortunately, Yemenis today seem more divided than ever. Deep gulfs separate the rich and poor, the urban and the rural, and the religious traditionalists and the religious moderates. As the political factions representing different interests battle one another, what lies ahead for this country is uncertain.

CHAPTER 2

Mountains and Deserts

YEMEN IS LOCATED ON THE SOUTHWESTERN TIP OF the Arabian Peninsula. Flanked by the Red Sea and the Arabian Sea, the peninsula lies in the portion of western Asia known as the Middle East. Most of the Arabian Peninsula is a sand-covered desert—so hot and dry that it can sustain only the hardiest forms of life. Much of Yemen is desert land. But the country also boasts high mountains, beautiful beaches, and valleys lush with vegetation. Because of its rich lands, the ancient Romans called the region Arabia Felix, or "Flourishing Arabia."

Despite its fertile lands, in one important way Yemen is the least fortunate country on the Arabian Peninsula. Unlike nearby Saudi Arabia, Qatar, and the United Arab Emirates, Yemen is not sitting on vast reserves of oil, which have made those nations extremely wealthy. With its modest oil reserves nearly depleted, Yemen is one of the poorest countries of the Middle East.

Opposite: **An old stone bridge connects two mountains at the village of Shaharah in northern Yemen.**

Yemen's Geographic Features

Area: 203,850 square miles (527,969 sq km)

Highest Elevation: 12,336 feet (3,760 m) above sea level, at Mount al-Nabi Shu'ayb

Lowest Elevation: Sea level along the coast

Average High Temperature: In Sanaa, 72°F (22°C) in January, 80°F (27°C) in July; in Aden, 82°F (28°C) in January, 97°F (36°C) in July

Average Low Temperature: In Sanaa, 37°F (3°C) in January, 56°F (13°C) in July; in Aden, 73°F (23°C) in January, 84°F (29°C) in July

Average Annual Precipitation: In Sanaa, 10 inches (25 cm); in Aden, 1.6 inches (4 cm)

Largest Island: Socotra, 1,409 square miles (3,650 sq km)

Longest Valley: Wadi Hadhramaut, about 400 miles (650 km)

Largest Man-made Lake: Marib Reservoir, 12 square miles (31 sq km)

Longest Border: With Saudi Arabia, 812 miles (1,307 km)

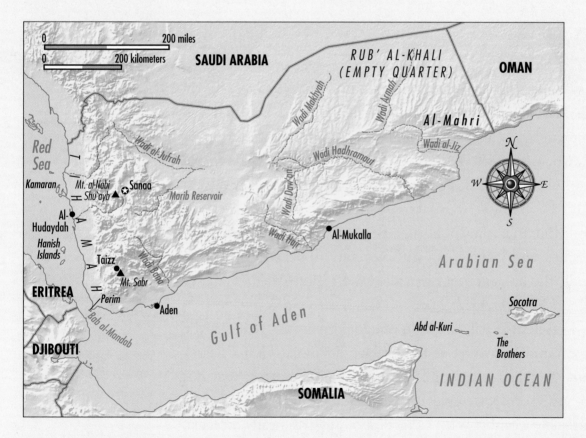

This satellite photo shows the Bab al-Mandab strait, which separates Africa from Asia. Yemen is the land at the top of the photo, and the African nations of Eritrea and Djibouti are at the bottom. At its narrowest point, Bab al-Mandab is just 18 miles (29 km) wide.

The Lay of the Land

Yemen shares a border with two nations—Saudi Arabia to the north and Oman to the east. To the south lies the Gulf of Aden, part of the Arabian Sea. To the west is the Red Sea. Connecting these two waterways is the strait of Bab al-Mandab, and on the other side of Bab al-Mandab are the African countries of Eritrea and Djibouti.

Bab al-Mandab means "gate of tears" in Arabic. The name probably came from the frustration sailors had in navigating their vessels through this narrow waterway. Many ships heading from Asia to Africa and back again still travel through Bab al-Mandab daily.

Yemen has an area of 203,850 square miles (527,969 square kilometers), making it a bit smaller than the U.S. state of Texas. Yemen's lands include about two hundred islands.

Among them are Kamaran and the Hanish Islands in the Red Sea and Perim in Bab al-Mandab. Yemen's largest island is Socotra, which is located in the Arabian Sea. For most of their history, the inhabitants of Socotra had only limited contact with outsiders, including other Yemenis. In recent years, Socotra has been a destination for adventurous tourists eager to see the island's diverse plants and animals and to enjoy surfing and snorkeling along its pristine beaches.

The geography and climate of Yemen varies greatly. But the country can be roughly divided into three geographic regions. Along the Red Sea is the coastal plain. In the east are the desert lands of the Empty Quarter. In the north and west are the highlands.

The waters off the island of Socotra are renowned for their turquoise color.

City Life

About 30 percent of Yemenis live in urban centers. The nation's largest city is the capital of Sanaa with a population of 2,833,000. Aden is home to more than 800,000 people, while Taizz and Al-Hudaydah each have populations of more than 400,000.

According to legend, Noah's ark was launched from the port of Aden. Located in southwestern Yemen along the Gulf of Aden, this ancient city was the capital of the People's Democratic Republic of Yemen (South Yemen) before Yemen became a united country in 1990. The oldest part of the city, called Crater, sits in an

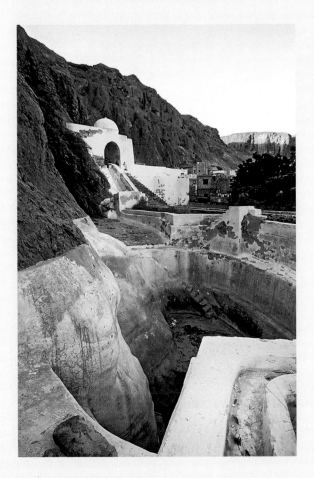

extinct volcano. Aden is known for its beautiful beaches. Among its historical landmarks are the Tawila Tanks (left), which were constructed at least one thousand years ago to collect water for the city.

Taizz (above) sits in Yemen's highlands at the foot of Mount Sabr. The city is home to al-Ashrafiya mosque, one of the earliest built in Yemen. It has also traditionally been the center of education in Yemen. Coffee is one of the leading industries in Taizz. Farmers there also grow vegetables, cotton, and a plant called khat, also spelled qat. Yemenis chew khat leaves when relaxing with friends.

Al-Hudaydah on the Tihamah coastal plain is an important port city. Its large fish market sells everything from the sea, from shrimp to shark meat. The city is a popular vacation spot for Yemenis, and visitors enjoy strolling through its many parks and along its seaside walkway.

A child on the coast in the Tihamah. In this region, people fish from colorful boats called dhows.

The Tihamah

The coastal plain of southern Yemen is known as the Tihamah, which appropriately means "hot earth." This flat, narrow, sandy plain is brutally hot and humid much of the year. During the summer, temperatures regularly rise above 100 degrees Fahrenheit (38 degrees Celsius). On particularly steamy days, the temperature can be as high as 130°F (54°C).

The region receives very little rain. The annual rainfall is only about 9 inches (23 centimeters), and Aden, the largest city on the coastal plain, usually experiences even less. Farmers in the Tihamah cannot rely on rain to water their crops. They instead must dig wells and pump up groundwater to irrigate their fields.

Living in this environment is always difficult, but it is especially so between May and October. During that time, strong winds blow up from the Red Sea, whirling sand and dust into the air. These sandstorms can be so severe that they block out the sun and darken the sky, making it impossible to see more than a few feet in any direction.

The Rub' al-Khali

The most forbidding environment in Yemen is found in the east. The area, called the Rub' al-Khali or "Empty Quarter," is part of the vast Arabian Desert. These desert lands make up about half of the country.

A sandstorm darkens the sky in Sanaa. Sandstorms can make it difficult to drive, and the tiny particles can damage the lungs of the people who breathe them.

True to its name, the Rub' al-Khali is virtually empty of humans and wildlife. The climate is punishingly hot, with temperatures frequently topping 120°F (49°C). It is also very dry, with no rainfall often for years at a time. Between the heat and the lack of water, it is impossible to grow crops in most of this region.

The few inhabitants of the Rub' al-Khali are Bedouins. Herders of camels and other livestock, many Bedouins do not live in permanent settlements. Instead, they live nomadically, moving from one grazing area to the next with their animals.

A truck drives across the dunes in the Rub' al-Khali, the largest sand desert in the world.

Water Worries

With each passing year, Yemen comes closer and closer to depleting one of its most important resources—fresh water.

Demand for water has grown with Yemen's population. Between 1960 and 2015, the number of Yemenis has jumped from five million to twenty-six million. To feed a population this size, Yemeni farmers can no longer rely on just rainwater to irrigate their fields. For decades, they have tapped into groundwater, but this source of water is almost gone.

Beginning in the 1980s, international organizations such as the World Bank promoted agricultural development in Yemen that encouraged farmers to grow vegetables and citrus fruit for export. These crops needed a lot of water. As this plan failed, many farmers

began growing more and more khat (above) to make up for their lost income. The roots of the khat shrub are very deep and thirsty. Today, about 40 percent of all fresh water available in Yemen is used to grow this crop.

The water shortage is already responsible for some of the violence that is tearing the country apart. Some groups in rural areas, for instance, routinely fight over water sources. The terrorist group al-Qaeda in the Arabian Peninsula also exploits people's fears of not having enough water to drink. The group often finds new recruits by giving them water or teaching them how to build a well.

Green fields cover the hillsides in the highlands near Taizz.

The Green Land

The highlands of Yemen stand in stark contrast to its desert. With a healthy annual rainfall and moderate climate, this region is full of natural vegetation and cultivated fields. Yemen is known as the Green Land of Arabia because of its fertile highlands.

The western highlands lie inland from the coastal plain. Much of the area is covered by flat-topped hills, but there are also mountains, which run parallel to the Red Sea. The great Mount al-Nabi Shuʻayb, whose peak rises to 12,336 feet (3,760 meters), is the highest point on the Arabian Peninsula. The central highlands to the east feature mountains, but they are not so tall.

The temperatures in the highlands are generally comfortably warm, although winter nights can be chilly. In the summer, high temperatures hover around 80°F (27°C). In the winter, they rise to only about 55°F (13°C).

Summer is the rainy season in the highlands. During this time, the region often sees more than 15 inches (38 cm) of rain, as winds carry moisture from the Indian Ocean. Highland farmers capture the rain in irrigation ditches. The ditches direct the water to their fields, which are located on terraces cut into the mountain slopes.

Summer rain also fills wadis, long valleys that turn into rivers during the rainy season. Water collected in the wadis is used to irrigate fields. Wadi Hadhramaut, the longest wadi in Yemen, stretches about 400 miles (650 kilometers). The surrounding land is the most fertile in the country. Through irrigation, farmers there grow vegetables, fruits, and grains, but the region is best known for its forests of date trees.

A Land of Giants

Legend holds that Wadi Hadhramaut was once home to giants. They were very wealthy and built beautiful cities, but they angered God for not thanking him for their good fortune. God punished them by unleashing a sandstorm and an army of enormous ants that tore the giants apart limb by limb.

CHAPTER 3

Wild Things

ACCORDING TO YEMENI LEGEND, SHEM, THE SON of Noah in the Bible, wandered the desert, looking for a place to build a great city. He found what he thought was the perfect spot. Shem laid a string on the ground, marking where he would construct the city's foundation. But then a bird suddenly came down from the sky, snatched the string in its beak, and flew away. Shem followed the bird, taking its appearance as a sign. When the bird flew to the ground and laid down the string, Shem realized the bird had steered him to just the right place. There, he built his settlement, which is today the site of Sanaa, Yemen's capital.

Unsurprisingly, this story of Yemen's origins highlights a creature from the natural world. Like other peoples, the Yemenis feel a deep connection to the animals and plants with which they share their lands.

Opposite: **An Egyptian vulture soars over Yemen. Egyptian vultures are easily identified by their bright yellow faces.**

Varied Habitats

Few creatures live in the eastern desert lands of Yemen. Only the hardy scorpion, some snakes, lizards, and a few insects can survive in its scorchingly hot and extremely dry climate.

The Tihamah on the coast of the Red Sea is almost as inhospitable. In this humid environment, there are plenty of mosquitoes but few other native animals. There is only sparse wild vegetation. However, in some areas, farmers use underground water sources to grow crops.

The highlands, in contrast, are teeming with life. With many trees and shrubs, the region is lush with vegetation. A

A scorpion skitters across the sand in the Rub' al-Khali. Scorpions are among the few creatures that can survive in the scorching desert.

wide variety of animals, large and small, are also found there. The highlands are home to gazelles, leopards, birds, lizards, snakes, butterflies, and many other types of animal life.

From the Earth

The plant life of the highlands includes more than six hundred types of flowering plants, including the tamarisk and ficus. The acacia bush found to the west is known for its small white and yellow flowers. The Yemenis use these flowers to create colorful dyes.

Many varieties of grapes grow in the highlands. Trees are also plentiful in the area. Some of these trees provide Yemenis with fruit such as mangoes, papayas, peaches, and apricots.

A Yemeni Delicacy

Bees in the region of Wadi Daw'an, in the central part of the county, produce one of the most prized taste treats in the world—Yemeni honey. These bees feed on the flowers of the Sidr tree—also known as Christ's thorn tree because the crown of thorns worn by Jesus in the Bible was supposedly made from this type of tree. Because of the bees' diet, their honey is extremely rich and flavorful. Sought out by connoisseurs of fine foods, it often sells for as much as one hundred times the cost of regular honey.

The most important fruit-bearing tree in Yemen is the date palm. These palms have deep roots that can tap into water sources far underground. They flourish particularly well along the Wadi Hadhramaut. Nutritious dates are an important part of the Yemeni diet. Yemen produces so many dates that it exports some to other Middle Eastern nations. The date palm's trunk provides timber, while the ribs of its leaves are used to make furniture and crates. Yemenis also weave the leaves to create baskets.

Along terraced hillsides and the banks of the wadis, Yemeni farmers grow a variety of crops. They include wheat, onions, beans, cotton, and khat. The Wadi Hadhramaut is well suited for growing coffee and tobacco.

Animal Life

Large wild mammals are most commonly found in Yemen's mountainous region. They include the mountain gazelle, the striped hyena, the Arabian wolf, and the ibex. The largest of these mammals is the hamadryas baboon, which is notable for its pink face and silvery mane.

Saving the Arabian Leopard

In April 2008, Yemen's Council of Ministers named the Arabian leopard the country's national animal. The declaration was made not only to celebrate this majestic animal, but also to save it. According to the Foundation for the Protection of the Arabian Leopard in Yemen, there are only between 100 and 250 Arabian leopards left in the wild.

One of nine subspecies of leopard, the Arabian leopard is distinguished by its pale coat and long tail, which helps the animal balance. Living in the mountains and along the wadis of Yemen, the Arabian leopard preys on the Nubian ibex and the mountain gazelle, but also feeds on smaller animals, including hares, foxes, and porcupines. By making the Arabian leopard a symbol of national pride, the Yemeni government hoped to protect the animal from its two greatest threats: animal herders, who sometimes shoot leopards when the large cats feed on their livestock, and trappers, who capture them to sell to collectors of exotic wild animals.

Camels are not as commonly found in Yemen as in some other Middle Eastern countries. Nomadic people in Yemen's desert, however, use camels to travel from place to place. Yemeni herders also raise sheep, cattle, and goats.

More than 360 species of birds—including hawks, vultures, parrots, and finches—are found in Yemen. Most do not live there year-round, but instead visit the area during their yearly migrations. In the highlands, reptiles are also common. They include snakes such as cobras and vipers, and lizards such as geckos and chameleons. Yemen boasts

A Yemeni boy holds a bag of locusts. Locusts often travel in huge swarms and can quickly devour crops as they sweep across the land.

more than one hundred species of butterflies. Among the thousands of other types of insects are beetles, locusts, millipedes, and spiders.

The Veiled Chameleon

The veiled chameleon is a favorite pet of reptile lovers. Native to Yemen and Saudi Arabia, the chameleon is a light green color when it is young. But as it matures, its body becomes covered with brilliant green, gold, and blue bands. Like other chameleons, it changes color to blend into its surroundings. In a tree or a bush, the veiled chameleon is invisible to the insects on which it feeds. Its eyes move independently from each other. Sitting still, it can easily spy nearby prey. With its long sticky tongue, it can capture an insect and snap it into its mouth in seconds. The "veil" that gives the animal its name is a helmetlike crest on its head. Sloping downward, it collects drops of rain that slide directly into the reptile's mouth.

The Island of Socotra

Yemen's most unusual wildlife is found on the island of Socotra. Located in the Indian Ocean about 210 miles (340 km) from the mainland, Socotra had little contact with the outside world until recently. Over millions of years, its plant life and animal life were left to slowly evolve so they could thrive in the island's misty mountains and dry lowlands. As a result, many of the species there are found nowhere else in the world.

Among the weird and wonderful plants of Socotra is the cucumber tree. It is the only plant of the cucumber family that can grow up to 20 feet (6 m) tall. Its thick trunk stores water so it can survive during periods of little rainfall.

Socotra is home to many unusual plants, including the cucumber tree.

Another distinctive plant of Socotra is the desert rose. Its name suggests the plant is a thing of beauty. But, with only slight exaggeration, one nineteenth-century visitor to Socotra declared it was "the ugliest tree in creation." From its misshapen stumpy trunk, branches stick out in all directions, topped by small purple flowers.

The desert rose tree can grow to 16 feet (5 m) tall. Delicate flowers grow from the top of its huge, bulbous trunk.

Nine out of ten reptile species of Socotra do not exist anywhere else. One unique species is the Socotran chameleon. Some Yemenis of Socotra say this reptile has magical powers. According to legend, if people hear its hiss, they lose the ability to speak.

The Socotran chameleon can change colors. Depending on the situation, it can be gray, brown, or green.

Saving Nature

For thousands of years, the people of Socotra were isolated from the outside world. But that has changed, largely because of Yemen's tourism industry. In 1999, only seventy tourists visited Socotra. By 2010, that number had risen to four thousand. These tourists, and the roads and hotels built to accommodate them, are placing stress on the natural environment. The lack of young dragon's blood trees—the peculiar mushroom-shaped trees that once covered much of the island—is evidence of this growing problem.

Dragon's Blood

The national tree of Yemen is the dragon's blood, one of the many biological wonders of the island of Socotra. The strange shape of its branches, which makes the tree look like an open umbrella, helps it take in moisture from the island's misty air. Its colorful name comes from its red sap, which Yemenis have long used to heal wounds. Recent scientific research suggests that the sap might have other medicinal uses, such as treating infections.

In an effort to preserve its unique plant and animal life, Yemen designated three-fourths of the island as national park-land. Socotra was also named a UNESCO (United Nations Educational, Scientific and Cultural Organization) World

Shepherds lead sheep and goats through dusty fields in the highlands.

Heritage Site in 2008. This ensures that the United Nations, an international organization, will provide funds to protect its habitat and wildlife.

Both male and female Arabian oryx have long, straight horns.

Many plants and animals on Yemen's mainland are also in danger. In recent years, the human population has grown rapidly. The habitats of some species have been destroyed with the building of new houses and roads. By allowing their livestock to overgraze on natural grasses, herders have also destroyed large swaths of land. Some animals, such as the Arabian oryx and several species of marine turtles, are endangered. Others, including the Queen of Sheba's gazelle, are already extinct. Yemen's government is aware of the threats to its natural wonders, but it is too early to tell whether the government will be able to act in time to save its endangered animals.

CHAPTER 4

Country in Conflict

PEOPLE HAVE INHABITED THE LAND THAT IS NOW Yemen for thousands of years. Beginning in about 1200 BCE, it was ruled by a series of ancient kingdoms, including those of the Himyarites, the Minaeans, and the Sabaeans. Encounters between the Sabaeans' ruler Bilqis (also known as the Queen of Sheba) and King Solomon are recorded in the Bible and in the Qur'an, the holy book of Islam.

These early kingdoms grew wealthy from trade. Southern Arabia lay along a route by which traders transported luxury goods loaded on caravans of camels. The goods included ivory from Africa, spices from India, and silk from China. The traders also peddled frankincense and myrrh, which were made from the resin of trees native to Yemen. Yemen prospered for nearly one thousand years before the Romans took over this trade network.

Opposite: **About four thousand years ago, the Sabaeans built a temple to the moon in Marib, in central Yemen. The massive columns are about four stories tall.**

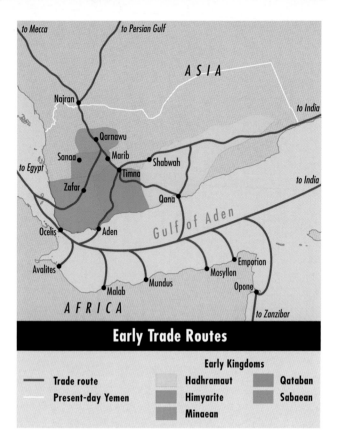

Early Trade Routes

Early Kingdoms

—— Trade route

—— Present-day Yemen

- Hadhramaut
- Himyarite
- Minaean
- Qataban
- Sabaean

Becoming Muslim

In 525 CE, Ethiopians invaded what is now Yemen. It remained under the control of the Ethiopian kingdom for fifty years, until it was taken over by Persians, people from the region that is now Iran. In 628, the Persian governor who ruled the region converted to a new religion—Islam. Islam was based on the teachings of a prophet named Muhammad, who lived in what is now Saudi Arabia. He told his followers to stop believing in multiple gods and instead worship the one true God,

Frankincense and Myrrh

Two of the most treasured trade goods in the ancient world were frankincense and myrrh. Both were made from the resin of small trees that grew in southern Arabia. When burned, frankincense produced a sweet-smelling smoke. The incense was an important part of religious ceremonies performed in Egypt, Mesopotamia, Greece, Rome, and Arabia. Myrrh was burned as incense as well, but it was also used to make perfumes and medicines. Because of the high demand for frankincense and myrrh, the cost of these goods was very high. In the Biblical story of the birth of Jesus, the three wise men offered the baby gold, frankincense, and myrrh. At the time, these were the most valuable gifts that money could buy.

Marib Dam

The kingdom of Saba constructed a great dam near its capital of Marib, perhaps as early as the eighth century BCE. Some historians call this great engineering feat the eighth wonder of the ancient world. The dam collected water during the rainy season. The Sabaeans used the water to irrigate their fields. Through irrigation, they could grow enough food for all of the people of Marib. The dam water also allowed trees in the region to thrive. Frankincense and myrrh were valuable trade goods that helped make Saba prosperous.

In the sixth century CE, the Great Dam of Marib collapsed. It may have been strained by particularly strong rains or destroyed in an earthquake. The dam's collapse contributed to the end of Saba. Without its waters and the agricultural products they produced, many Sabaeans were forced to leave the region.

which is "Allah" in Arabic. At the demand of the Persian governor, the people of southern Arabia became Muslims, believers in Islam. The region then was known as Yemen, which means "the right side" in Arabic. Muslims believed Yemen was on the right side of the Arabian Peninsula because it was the side closest to Mecca, the holy city where Muhammad had been born.

In the late ninth century, north Yemen came under the control of a powerful Muslim leader, Yahya bin al-Husayn bin al-Qasim ar-Rassi, who was able to broker a peace among warring groups. By then, followers of Islam had split into two groups—Shi'is and Sunnis. Al-Qasim ar-Rassi was a Shi'i who belonged to the Zaydi sect. The Zaydis called their leaders imams. Well into the twentieth century, Zaydi imams held power in Yemen's northern reaches.

Enter the Turks

In 1530s and 1540s, the Turks of the Ottoman Empire took over much of Yemen. The Turks increased trade in the region. European traders were particularly eager to obtain coffee beans grown in the highlands.

The Zaydi imams were restored to power in the 1630s, but the Turks still held sway in the region. By the mid-nineteenth century, the Ottoman Turks had regained control in North Yemen in hopes of countering the influence the British had over South Yemen.

Two Queens

While accepting the Nobel Peace Prize in 2011, Yemeni activist Tawakkol Karman celebrated her country as the "land of two queens." She was referring to two of Yemen's most famous historical leaders—Bilqis and Arwa.

Bilqis (far right), also known as the Queen of Sheba, ruled what are now Yemen and Ethiopia in the tenth century BCE. Her meeting with King Solomon (right) of Israel is recounted in both the Bible and the Qur'an. In the Qur'an, she travels to Solomon's palace, where he persuades her to worship one god.

Born in 1045 CE, Arwa ruled southern Arabia for more than fifty years. The queen was known for her generosity and for her knowledge of poetry and the Qur'an. She moved the capital to Jiblah, where she built a large mosque. Today the mosque is a popular tourist attraction.

The British taking possession of Aden. The British established a military base at Aden and used the city as a stopping point where its steam-powered ships could be resupplied with coal.

Controlling Aden

For centuries, foreigners had tried to gain a foothold in South Yemen. They were particularly interested in the port city of Aden because of the shipping traffic there. After several failed attempts, the British finally succeeded in capturing Aden in 1839. Control of the port was particularly important to the British because they wanted to protect their shipping route to and from India, which the British then ruled. At Aden, they established a station where British ships could stop and refuel.

Wanting to ensure that the Turks did not make any inroads into the area around the port, the British made agreements with local people near Aden. They promised the local lead-

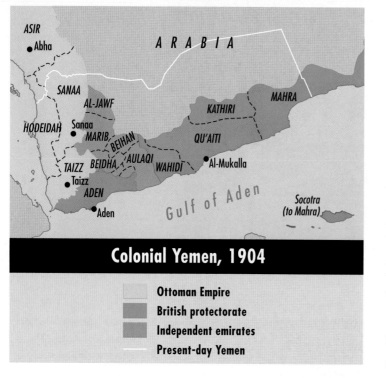

Colonial Yemen, 1904

ASIR
Abha
ARABIA
SANAA
AL-JAWF
KATHIRI
MAHRA
HODEIDAH
Sanaa
MARIB
BEIHAN
QU'AITI
TAIZZ
BEIDHA
AULAQI
WAHIDI
Al-Mukalla
Taizz
ADEN
Aden
Gulf of Aden
Socotra
(to Mahra)

- Ottoman Empire
- British protectorate
- Independent emirates
- Present-day Yemen

ers military protection against their enemies if they pledged loyalty to Britain. The areas that came under British rule became known as the Aden Protectorate. While controlled by Britain, Aden grew and prospered, becoming a significant center for trade.

The Ottoman Turks in the north and the British in the south repeatedly clashed until they agreed on a border separating the north from the south in 1904. By that time, the Zaydi leaders were weary of Turkish rule. Their followers staged a series of uprisings. After the Turks lost World War I (1914–1918), they realized they no longer had the power to hold on to North Yemen. The Turks withdrew from the region.

Under Zaydi Rule

In 1918, a Zaydi imam named Yahya bin Muhammad Hamid al-Din saw the opportunity to extend his power. Battling political rivals, he took control of North Yemen. Imam Yahya also successfully defended his rule during a brief war with Saudi Arabia in 1934. During his reign, Imam Yahya tried to isolate North Yemen from foreigners. He also worked to improve the country's agricultural production so it would not have to rely on exports from other nations.

Dar al-Hajar

In the 1930s, Imam Yahya had a summer palace built outside the city of Sanaa. Called the Dar al-Hajar, this brown house decorated with white latticework sits on top of a high rock overlooking the fertile Wadi Dhahr. Because of this, it is sometimes called the Rock Palace. With its dramatic architecture, Dar al-Hajar has become a symbol of Yemen.

Imam Yahya was a harsh ruler. Some Yemenis strongly opposed him. Among them was a group known as al-Ahrar al-Yamaniyyin (Free Yemenis). They wanted to see reforms

Imam Yahya and his son. Imam Yahya tried to isolate Yemen from the rest of the world. He wanted no foreign influences in the country.

in the government to transform North Yemen into a more modern nation. They assassinated Imam Yahya in 1948 and tried to take over North Yemen. The group was challenged by Yahya's son Ahmad and his followers. Backed by Saudi Arabia, Ahmad seized control and became his father's successor.

Ahmad did not hesitate to use violence to maintain power. His strong-armed tactics earned him many enemies. His own brother Abdullah joined with the army to bring

Muhammad al-Badr (left) helped put down the revolt against his father, Imam Ahmad. Muhammad later served briefly as imam before being forced into exile.

down Ahmad's government in 1955. This military coup failed, and Abdullah was executed.

The Yemen Arab Republic

In 1962, Ahmad died in his sleep. His son Muhammad al-Badr became north Yemen's new leader, but his rule lasted only a few days. The army once again conspired to take over the nation, and this time it succeeded. Military officials ousted al-Badr and replaced him with army colonel Abdullah al-Sallal. The country was renamed the Yemen Arab Republic (YAR).

The power play sparked a civil war. Still supported by Zaydi people, al-Badr fielded an army and tried to retake the country. His cause was supported by Saudi Arabia and Great Britain. Al-Sallal's followers received aid from Egypt and the Soviet Union, a large country made up of Russia and many other now-independent countries in Asia and Europe.

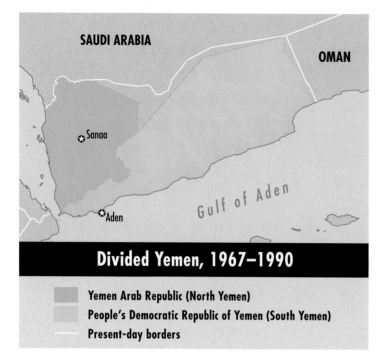

SAUDI ARABIA

OMAN

Sanaa

Aden

Gulf of Aden

Divided Yemen, 1967–1990

Yemen Arab Republic (North Yemen)
People's Democratic Republic of Yemen (South Yemen)
Present-day borders

With modern arms and machinery from these foreign countries, the war was drawn-out and extremely bloody. Overwhelmed by its own war with Israel, Egypt pulled out its troops in 1967. With the loss of this vital ally, al-Sallal seemed sure to lose. But after three more years of fighting, his forces defeated those of the imam. Al-Badr spent the rest of his life in exile in Britain.

The People's Democratic Republic of Yemen

During this period, South Yemen was also in political chaos. In 1962, the British-held territory there became known as the Federation of South Arabia. By that time, the British no longer had the means to control far-flung nations such as India and South Yemen. They planned to establish a representative government in Yemen before withdrawing, but rival Yemeni factions began fighting with each other and with the British. When the British left in 1967, one group, the National Liberation Front, emerged victorious. It declared that the People's Republic of South Yemen was now an independent country. After another power struggle, the nation was reconfigured as the People's Democratic Republic of Yemen (PDRY) in 1970.

PDRY was a communist country. Under this political structure, the government owned the nation's businesses. PDRY received aid and support from the Soviet Union, then the largest communist country in the world. Even so, the new nation struggled economically. Still trying to recover from war, it also saw its income from trade rapidly decline. The PDRY tried to force Britain to compensate it for Britain's long occupation of South Yemen. But Britain offered only a small payment, far less than what the PDRY needed. Even so, the country had a good educational system, and the rate of literacy, the ability to read and write, among women improved dramatically.

Aden in 1972. The city served as the capital of South Yemen.

During the 1970s, the PDRY fought two border wars with the YAR. But at the same time, the two Yemens also began discussing the possibility of uniting. Discussions stalled, however, in part because of a brief civil war among rival factions in the PDRY in 1986.

The Soviet Union began a youth group called the Young Pioneers, which was similar to the Boy Scouts but also taught communist ideals. Children in the People's Democratic Republic of Yemen also joined the Young Pioneers.

A United Yemen

Within a few years, the idea of a united Yemen was revived. The economy of YAR had stabilized under Ali Abdullah Saleh, who had succeeded in calming rival groups there after becom-

ing president in 1978. The financial situation in the PDRY, however, had grown dire. The Soviet Union collapsed in 1989, so the PDRY lost its most important source of foreign aid. Being absorbed into a united Yemen seemed the PDRY's best hope for survival. A united Yemen also seemed better positioned to profit from oil that had been discovered there in the 1980s.

Finally, on May 22, 1990, the two Yemens became one. The new country was named the Republic of Yemen. Ali Abdullah Saleh, the former president of the YAR, was named its president. Ali Salim al-Bayd, a politician in the PDRY, became its vice president.

During the first few years after Yemen united, the press enjoyed greater freedom than it had ever had before in the country. People had greater freedom to speak their minds, and organizations could work to improve the country.

Ali Abdullah Saleh (right) of the Yemen Arab Republic joins hands with Ali Salim a-Bayd of the People's Democratic Republic of Yemen at the unification ceremony of the two Yemens in 1990.

Yemeni men await transport back to their home country after being forced to leave Saudi Arabia.

But Yemen also faced many difficulties after unification. In 1991, the United States and its allies declared war on Iraq because it had invaded the neighboring nation of Kuwait. Yemen did not support the war. To punish Yemen's government, Saudi Arabia, a U.S. ally, expelled as many as one million Yemeni workers who had been living in Saudi Arabia. The workers could not easily find jobs in Yemen. This large influx of newly unemployed people put an enormous strain on Yemen's economy.

Old rivalries also posed a threat to the Republic of Yemen. In May 1994, a faction in the south declared that its followers were seceding, or breaking away, to form a new country. For months, Saleh's forces battled the secessionists before defeating them. The victory ensured that Yemen would remain a single country for at least the near future. But many of the freedoms that had been established only a few years earlier were now reduced.

Opposing Saleh

In 1999, Saleh became the first directly elected president of Yemen. He was reelected in 2006. But by then his government was dealing with another rebellion—this time by a group of Zaydi Shi'is in the northwest called the Houthis. The army battled the Houthis, sometimes with the help of forces from Saudi Arabia. The two sides reached a cease-fire in 2010.

At that time, though, the government was dealing with two other enemies within its borders. In 2008, the southern secession movement was revived. And in 2009, the terrorist group al-Qaeda in the Arabian Peninsula (AQAP) was

In 1999, Ali Abdullah Saleh was directly elected president of Yemen for the first time. By this time, he had already been the leader of Yemen or North Yemen for twenty-one years.

The Saleh Mosque

The Saleh Mosque, named after President Ali Abdullah Saleh, opened in Sanaa in 2008. The mosque has become one of Yemen's most famous attractions. It is the largest mosque in the country, with a main hall that can hold forty-five thousand worshipers. Its six minarets are each more than 328 feet (100 m) tall, which is taller than a thirty-story building. These towers rise so high in the air that they are equipped with lights to warn passing airplanes of their presence. The mosque also features lush carpets, stained glass windows, and crystal chandeliers.

The only mosque in Yemen that is open to non-Muslims, the Saleh Mosque is popular with foreign tourists. Many Yemenis also enjoy visiting the grounds and having picnics in the nearby flower gardens. Since the 2011 revolution, however, the mosque has become controversial. Many people have criticized former president Ali Abdullah Saleh for spending lavishly on its construction, while most Yemenis live in poverty. During the revolution, activists started calling the building the People's Mosque, because they did not want the landmark to stand as a tribute to Saleh and his regime.

formed. The Saleh government received billions of dollars in aid from the United States to combat the menace of AQAP. Another branch of al-Qaeda had been responsible for the bombing of the USS *Cole*, a U.S. Navy ship, in Yemen in 2000. Al-Qaeda was also behind the terrorist attacks in the United States on September 11, 2001.

Many ordinary Yemenis were also discontent under Saleh's rule. His government was notoriously corrupt. Much of the country's wealth ended up in the hands of a small elite group made up of the president's relatives and close associates. While they lived in luxury, most Yemenis struggled to get by. Facing futures constrained by poverty and unemployment, young people were especially angry with Saleh.

A missile launched by al-Qaeda tore a huge hole in the side of the USS *Cole* during an attack in 2000. The attack killed or injured more than fifty people.

Police officers separate supporters and opponents of the government who clashed in Tahrir Square in 2011.

During the early months of 2011, people in many Arab countries took to the streets to demand that their governments serve all the people, not just the wealthy. This antigovernment protest movement became known as the Arab Spring. In Yemen, young people gathered daily in Sanaa's Tahrir Square, calling for Saleh to step down. Saleh's security forces attacked the protesters, but that only made them shout louder for the end of his presidency.

A New President

After surviving an attempt by al-Qaeda to assassinate him, Saleh bowed to the protesters' demands. In November 2011, he signed an agreement negotiated by the Gulf Cooperation Council. This organization, made up of representatives of six Middle Eastern countries, thought that if Saleh were peacefully removed from power, Yemen could avoid a civil war. By signing the agreement, Saleh resigned the presidency and agreed that Yemen's vice president, Abdu Rabbu Mansour Hadi, would become the new acting president.

A presidential election was scheduled for February 2012. Beforehand, the many political factions in Yemen agreed that Hadi should remain in power. He was elected president after running as the only candidate.

From the start, Hadi struggled in his new leadership role. Saleh had famously compared ruling Yemen to "dancing on the heads of snakes." He was referring to the seemingly impossible

Abdu Rabbu Mansour Hadi served as vice president for eight years before becoming president.

task of keeping control over the country's many rival political groups. Throughout his presidency, Saleh displayed astute political instincts, allowing him to play all these competing interests against one another. Without the social and political skills of Saleh, the shy and unassuming Hadi had trouble securing the loyalty of the various Yemeni political groups. He had a particularly strained relationship with the military after dismissing Saleh's relatives from high-ranking posts within it.

The Rise of the Houthis

Under Hadi's government, both AQAP and the southern secessionist movement grew stronger. But the greatest threat proved to be the Houthis in the north. By mid-2012, they controlled three governorates (regional governments similar to U.S. states) and prepared to take even more territory. In September 2014, Houthi forces advanced to the capital of Sanaa. After capturing the city, they dissolved Yemen's government and replaced it with their own. The rebels held Hadi under house arrest and forced him to resign. In February 2015, he escaped to the port of Aden and took back his resignation from the presidency. When Houthi forces reached Aden in late March, he fled the country, finding refuge in Saudi Arabia.

In Aden, two sides emerged, each made up of unlikely allies. The Houthis were joined by members of the military still loyal to Saleh, even though Saleh's forces had battled the Houthis during his presidency. Soldiers loyal to Hadi were aided by southern secessionists who earlier had been hostile to the national government. Also battling the Houthis were ordinary citizens who took to the streets determined to protect their city. Each side also had foreign allies who threatened to escalate the conflict into a regional war. Iran supported the Houthis, while Saudi Arabia aided Hadi's soldiers.

The day after Hadi's escape, Saudi Arabia began a series of air strikes that left much of Aden in ruins. With none of the combatants willing to negotiate, a solution to the crisis appeared nowhere in sight. During this violent time, Yemenis suffered as supplies of food, water, and fuel ran short. Only time will tell what the future holds for the people of this ancient land.

In 2014, Yemeni soldiers who supported the Houthi movement took to the streets in a demonstration demanding that the national government be replaced.

CHAPTER 5

Governing Yemen

THE STRUCTURE OF YEMEN'S GOVERNMENT WAS established in the country's constitution. The constitution was first adopted in 1991 and was later amended several times, most recently in 2009.

Three Branches

The constitution divides Yemen's government into three branches—the executive, the legislative, and the judicial. The president, elected by popular vote, is the head of the executive branch. The elected candidate serves a seven-year term. All citizens over age eighteen are allowed to vote.

The president chooses the vice president and the prime minister, who oversees the day-to-day operations of the

Yemen's Flag

The flag of Yemen features three horizontal bands—red on top, white in the middle, and black at the bottom. It was adopted in 1990 when North Yemen and South Yemen came together to form the Republic of Yemen. The red band stands for the blood shed during these struggles. The white band symbolizes the bright future all wanted for the new united Yemen. The black band represents the nation's history of conflict.

government. Also assisting the president is the Council of Ministers. Each minister is appointed by the president to provide advice about a specific aspect of government, such as foreign affairs or legal affairs.

The legislative branch makes laws. The lawmaking body is the parliament, which also approves treaties negotiated with other nations. Parliament is composed of the Shura Council and the House of Representatives. The president appoints the 111 members of the Shura Council. Voters elect the 301 members of the House of Representatives to six-year terms.

Heading the judicial branch is the Supreme Court, which is made up of about fifty judges. The court is organized into divisions, each of which hears only certain types of cases. The divisions include courts for constitutional, civil, criminal, military, and family cases. Judges in Yemen are religious scholars because the legal code is based on Islamic law, known as sharia (God's way). Below the Supreme Court are appeals courts, which review the decisions of lower courts, and courts of first instance, where cases are first heard.

Yemen's National Government

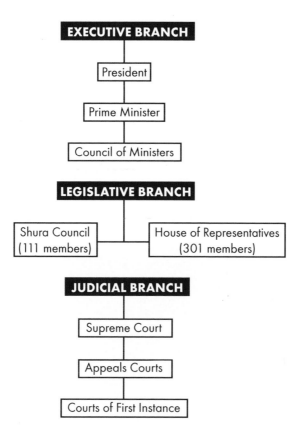

EXECUTIVE BRANCH

President

Prime Minister

Council of Ministers

LEGISLATIVE BRANCH

Shura Council
(111 members)

House of Representatives
(301 members)

JUDICIAL BRANCH

Supreme Court

Appeals Courts

Courts of First Instance

Local Government

Yemen is divided into twenty-one governorates, or *muhafazat*, each led by a governor. The governorates are further divided into more than three hundred districts, which are governed by local councils. The councils deal with health and educational issues. They also collect taxes.

In rural areas, the most important leaders are the heads of local groups. Local leaders resolve disputes among local group members and between groups. In some cases, they raise an army to fight a rival group. Some Yemenis feel much more loyalty to their local group and leader than they do to their country and its president.

Rewriting the Constitution

For its first thirty-three years, the Republic of Yemen had only one president—Ali Abdullah Saleh. He managed to hold the country together by playing various political groups against each other. He also paid bribes to buy votes and secure the support of local leaders.

Ali Abdullah Saleh in 1987. He was a colonel in the military before becoming president of North Yemen in 1977.

National Anthem

The music for the national anthem of Yemen, "United Republic," was written by Yemeni singer and musician Ayoob Tarish. The melody was paired with a patriotic poem written by Abdullah Abdulwahab Noman, who, like Tarish, was a native of the city of Taizz. The lyrics celebrate Yemen's heroes and its independence from the control of foreign countries. The song had been the anthem of the People's Democratic Republic of Yemen and was adopted as the anthem of the whole country when the two parts of Yemen united in 1990.

English translation
Repeat, O World, my song.
Echo it over and over again.
Remember, through my joy, each martyr.
Clothe him with the shining mantles
Of our festival.

Repeat, O World, my song.
In faith and love I am part of mankind.
An Arab I am in all my life.
My heart beats in tune with Yemen.
No foreigner shall dominate over Yemen.

الإرادة الثورية

Antigovernment protesters demanding the resignation of President Ali Abdullah Saleh filled the streets of Sanaa in 2011.

In addition to revolting in 2011 because of these abuses of power by Saleh, young Yemenis also protested his efforts to amend the constitution to make himself president for life, with his son Ahmed in place to succeed him. Saleh repeatedly promised to step down, yet he did so only under pressure from the Gulf Cooperation Council (GCC). The organization persuaded Saleh to resign, promising him that he would not be prosecuted for any crimes. By the arrangement, the vice president, Abdu Rabbu Mansour Hadi, became the new president.

In the aftermath of these changes, Yemeni leaders hashed out guidelines for a new type of government and wrote a new constitution. Under the new constitution, the president would serve a five-year term, and no one could hold this position for more than two terms. The constitution also outlawed political parties that were confined to members of specific ethnic groups or people with particular religious views. It also banned parties from forming armed militias.

Abdu Rabbu Mansour Hadi looks on during his presidential inauguration as former president Ali Abdullah Saleh holds the national flag.

A Look at the Capital

Located in Yemen's western highlands, Sanaa is the fastest-growing capital city in the world. Its population now tops 2.8 million. It is also one of the world's oldest cities, having been inhabited for some 2,500 years.

Sanaa means "fortified place." A high stone wall surrounds the oldest part of the city. This area is known for its tower houses. These old houses, six to eight stories tall, have been called the first skyscrapers. They are made of stone and clay brick.

Residents of Sanaa buy food and other goods at the Souq al-Milh, a huge open-air marketplace. The city is also the site of the Great Mosque, which has a library that contains the largest collection of Islamic manuscripts in Yemen. The government is a major employer in Sanaa. The city is also a center of trade.

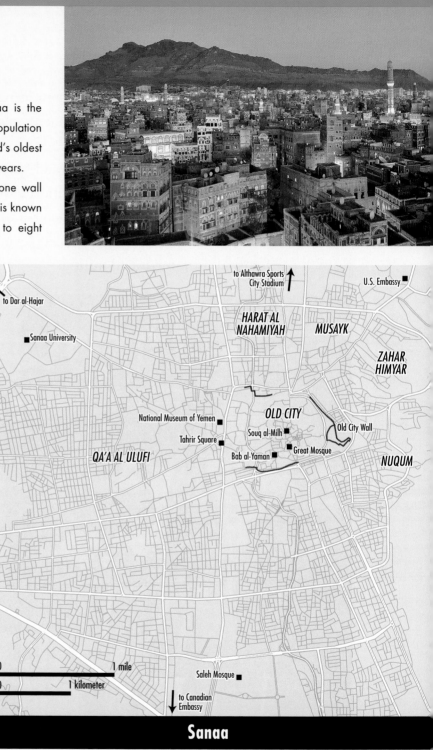

Sanaa

The Houthis' Government

The draft of the constitution was unveiled on January 17, 2015. The government hoped that it would reassure the world that Yemen was politically stable and open to reform. But by that time Yemen was in such political chaos that there was no possibility of the constitution being implemented.

The Houthis soon took over the government and announced they had dissolved Yemen's parliament. Ignoring the new constitution, the rebel group established the Revolutionary Committee, headed by Mohammed Ali al-Houthi, to create a new transitional government for Yemen. Other factions in Yemen, as well as most other nations (including the United States and Canada), do not recognize the Houthi government as legitimate. They still see Hadi, the last elected president, as Yemen's rightful leader.

Although not elected, Mohammed Ali al-Houthi (center) became, in effect, the leader of Yemen in 2015.

CHAPTER 6

A Struggling Economy

IN ANCIENT TIMES, WHAT IS NOW YEMEN WAS ONE of the most prosperous regions in the world. But modern Yemen has always been mired in poverty. One of the poorest nations in the Middle East, it has struggled with two obstacles to building a healthy economy.

The first is its geography. Unlike many other Middle Eastern countries, it has limited oil reserves, and those it does have are being rapidly depleted. Even though Yemen is home to the most fertile areas on the Arabian Peninsula, only about 3 percent of its lands can be farmed, leaving many Yemenis in a daily struggle to get enough food to eat.

The second obstacle is Yemen's history. Before Yemen was a unified country, the region in the north was ruled by imams who were not interested in investing in modern industries. After the Yemen Arab Republic was formed there, civil war kept its economy from growing. In the south, the People's Democratic Republic of Yemen suffered as Aden lost its place

Opposite: **A man sells peanuts at a market in Al-Hudaydah.**

as a major trading center. The country had to rely on funds from the Soviet Union for its survival. By 1990, the Yemenis hoped that, through unification, their combined government would be able to better exploit the country's supply of oil. But the government proved to be so corrupt that only a small elite profited from the oil revenue. Today, most Yemenis live in poverty, with nearly half getting by on the equivalent of US$2 a day.

Farming, Herding, and Fishing

Agriculture has long been central to Yemen's economy. Most Yemenis make their living through farming or by tending livestock. Many farms are found in the highlands. The fields are built on terraces cut into hillsides. These terraces provide flat land and keep the topsoil from washing away during heavy rains.

Yemenis also farm the fertile lands along wadis, valleys that collect rainwater. Yemen's largest wadi, Wadi Hadhramaut, is surrounded by land so rich and well-watered that almost anything can grow there. Farmers also live in the coastal plains. There, water pumped up from underground is used to irrigate fields.

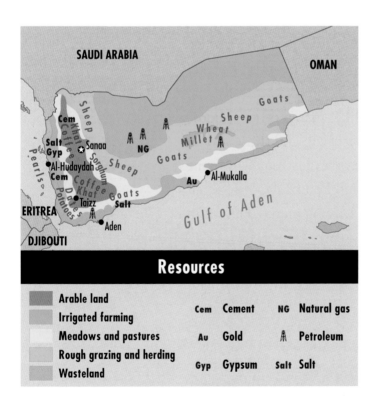

Resources

Arable land		
Irrigated farming	Cem Cement	NG Natural gas
Meadows and pastures	Au Gold	A Petroleum
Rough grazing and herding	Gyp Gypsum	Salt Salt
Wasteland		

The nation's most valuable crop is khat, a plant that has a mild stimulant like the caffeine in coffee. Yemen's farms also produce many types of fruits and vegetables, including apricots, mangoes, guavas, potatoes, onions, leeks, and tomatoes. Grains grown in Yemen include wheat, alfalfa, and barley, although sorghum is the most popular. Cotton and tobacco are important nonfood crops.

The highland region of Yemen is known for its coffee. Traditionally, it was shipped out of the port of Mocha. In English, the word *mocha* was originally used to describe very high quality coffee from the port. Now, mocha more often refers to coffee flavored with chocolate.

A farmer plows his land using a donkey. More than three-quarters of the labor force in Yemen works in agriculture.

Growing Khat

Increasingly, the most important crop grown in Yemen is khat. This shrub produces leaves that, when chewed, release a stimulant that makes people more talkative. Many Yemenis get together with friends every afternoon to talk and chew khat.

Demand for khat is high. This pushes prices up, making it profitable for farmers. Increasingly, Yemeni farmers have turned to growing khat, which produces several problems. Khat requires a great deal of water to grow, so it contributes to the broader problem of Yemen rapidly running out of fresh water. Devoting so much precious farmland to khat also means that Yemen cannot grow enough food to feed itself. Yemen has to import sugar, grain, flour, and many other foodstuffs from foreign countries.

Khat's popularity is also creating economic and social problems in Yemen. Families, even those living in poverty, often spend a large part of the household income on khat. Some economists fret over the many working hours lost to people spending their afternoons chewing khat.

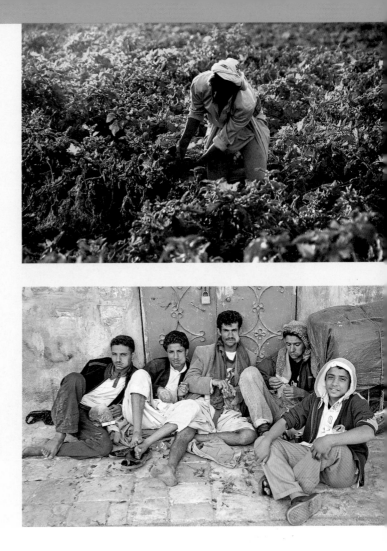

In rural areas, Yemenis raise a variety of animals. Some keep camels and donkeys and ride them as their primary form of transportation. Others tend herds of sheep and goats, which provide milk, hides, and wool. They raise cattle for their meat and chickens for their eggs.

Many Yemenis on the southern coast and on the island of Socotra fish for a living. They use their own small rafts or boats to sail into the Arabian and Red Seas. There, they catch mackerel, cuttlefish, shrimp, and lobster to sell at local markets.

What Yemen Grows, Makes, and Mines

AGRICULTURE

Sorghum (2012)	459,241 metric tons
Potatoes (2012)	294,686 metric tons
Khat (2011)	180,630 metric tons

MANUFACTURING (2009)

Petroleum products	4,222,000 metric tons
Cement and bricks	34,000 metric tons
Metal Products	23,000 metric tons

MINING (2011)

Oil	56,400,000 barrels
Gypsum	100,000 metric tons
Salt	75,000 metric tons

Industry

Some Yemeni workers hold factory jobs in cities. These factories make clothing, processed food, soap, perfume, and soft drinks. Factories also produce building materials, such as cement and bricks.

A few Yemenis earn their living by making traditional crafts. These include jewelry, wooden chests, and *jambiyas*. Jambiyas are decorative daggers with curved blades. Yemeni men wear them tucked into their belts.

Service Industries

Growing numbers of Yemenis work in service jobs. This includes teachers, restaurant employees, and people who work in sales.

Before the recent outbreak of violence, Yemen was trying to build its tourism industry. Few foreigners had ever traveled to Yemen, so growing numbers of tourists, particularly adventurous ones, were interested in visiting. Yemen was also a fairly inexpensive destination for North American and European travelers. To profit from tourism in Yemen, investors built restaurants, shops, and luxury hotels in Sanaa and Aden. They also constructed roads and resorts on Socotra. The island attracted vacationers interested in seeing its exotic trees and plants. Socotra's white beaches and coral reefs also made it a destination for surfers and scuba divers.

Tourists hike spectacular Mount Bura, which rises abruptly from the Tihamah region. The unrest of recent years has ended almost all tourism in Yemen.

Oil and Gas

The most lucrative industry in Yemen is the oil industry. Oil was first discovered in the country in the 1980s. Since that time, oil wealth has been the primary source of funds for the national government. By 2010, it accounted for 70 percent of all government revenue. The oil resources of Yemen, however, are meager in comparison to those of nearby oil-rich countries such as Saudi Arabia and the United Arab Emirates. In fact, Yemen will likely not have any oil left in a few years.

The government has looked for a replacement for the oil revenue. One possibility is to exploit the country's reserves of natural gas. In 2009, Yemen began exporting liquefied natural gas in an effort to diversify its economy. It is also trying to take advantage of its deposits of copper, gold, silver, zinc, cobalt, and other minerals.

A worker checks equipment at an oil plant in Wadi Hadhramaut. Oil and natural gas make up about one-quarter of Yemen's gross domestic product, the total value of all goods and services produced in the country.

In Yemen, the basic unit of currency is the rial. The government's central bank issues four coins worth 1, 5, 10, and 20 rials. Its banknotes come in six denominations: 50, 100, 200, 250, 500, and 1,000 rials. Each note has a distinctive color scheme so that the bills are easy to tell apart. For instance, bills worth 100 rials are red, purple, and orange, while bills worth 500 rials are blue, green, and pink. The writing on the bills is in Arabic on the front and in English on the back. Both sides of the bills bear images of Yemeni landmarks, artwork, or city scenes. The landmarks pictured include the Saleh Mosque (250 rials), Dar al-Hajar (500 rials), and the Bab al-Yaman gate on the wall surrounding old Sanaa (1,000 rials). In 2015, 10 rials equaled 5 U.S. cents, and US$1 was worth 215 Yemeni rials.

Economic Outlook

For decades, Yemen's economy has been propped up by aid from foreign countries. International organizations, including the World Bank and the International Monetary Fund, have also provided Yemen with substantial aid annually. But this has not been enough to lift the Yemeni people out of poverty.

The Yemeni protesters who took to the streets in 2011 were eager to see economic as well as political reforms. They experienced day-to-day the economic hardships of living under the corrupt Saleh regime. Many were unemployed. Others were students who had no chance of finding a job after graduating.

The protesters hoped that with Saleh removed from the presidency, Yemen's poor economy would improve. But instead his ouster created a power vacuum that led Yemen's many political factions to turn on one another. During these conflicts, normal economic activity all but ground to a halt, plunging an already poor people into desperation. As the fighting continued, getting food, medical attention, fuel, or any other basic necessity became more and more difficult. Demands for reform have been forgotten, at least temporarily, in the struggle to survive the war. Until the fighting stops, Yemen's economic situation is likely to only grow worse.

Women in Sanaa carry cans filled with water. International organizations are working to provide food and water to the people of Yemen.

CHAPTER 7

The People of Yemen

NEARLY ALL YEMENIS SHARE THE SAME ETHNICITY. About 92 percent of the twenty-six million Yemenis are Arabs. About 6 percent, most living along the coast of the Red Sea, are of mixed Arab and African descent. There is a small number of non-Arabs living in Yemen, most of whom are foreigners from European or South Asian countries.

Age and Class

By world standards, the population of Yemen is very young. About 41 percent of Yemenis are under fifteen years old. A full two-thirds of the population is under twenty-four. The country's high birth rate is in part responsible for the large percentage of young people. The average Yemeni woman has four children. Lack of health care and poor nutrition are also factors. Few Yemenis live long, healthy lives. Only 3 percent of them are sixty-five or older.

Ethnic Groups in Yemen	
Arab	91.7%
African-Arab	6.3%
South Asian, European, other	2.0%

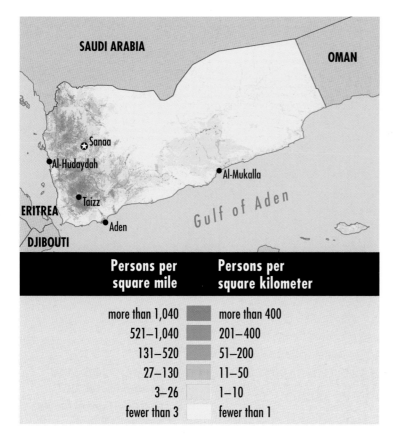

Persons per square mile		Persons per square kilometer
more than 1,040		more than 400
521–1,040		201–400
131–520		51–200
27–130		11–50
3–26		1–10
fewer than 3		fewer than 1

Population of Major Cities (2010 est.)

Sanaa	2,833,000
Aden	855,000
Taizz	467,000
Al-Hudaydah	410,000
Al-Mukalla	182,500

In recent years, many Yemenis have moved to cities, especially Sanaa, to find work. But the majority of Yemenis are still rural people. More than two-thirds of them live outside of urban areas, in villages or small towns. The Bedouin people were traditionally nomads, traveling through the desert from place to place. Some still live this way, but others live in permanent villages and work in oil fields. Bedouin people make up about 1 percent of Yemen's population.

The social class Yemenis come from affects where they live and what they do. People with an education hold positions in fields such as teaching and government work. They usually live and work in cities. The next highest social rank is craftspeople, followed by farmers. At the very bottom of society are laborers, called the Akhdam. They are confined to menial jobs and live in urban slums.

Speaking Arabic

For some two thousand years, the people of the Arabian Peninsula have spoken the Arabic language. It is the official language of Yemen.

The Akhdam

The lowest class in Yemen is composed of the Akhdam, or "servants." They call themselves al-Muhamasheen, or "marginalized people," because they are confined to the margins of Yemeni society.

The origins of the Akhdam are uncertain. But many believe they are the descendants of Ethiopians who invaded present-day Yemen some 1,500 years ago. Today, fellow Yemenis treat the Akhdam with disdain. The Akhdam are not allowed to rent or buy homes. Instead, they are forced to live in shacks in filthy slums outside cities, particularly Sanaa. No one will hire them to work jobs that pay a decent rate. To survive, they beg, sweep streets, and sift through mounds of garbage looking for scraps of metal they can sell. With no access to education and health care, they suffer from malnutrition and disease. One out of every nine Akhdam babies dies in infancy.

Some Akhdam are overwhelmed by hopelessness, sure nothing will ever change their lot in life. But others have taken to the streets to protest their treatment. No longer willing to live on the margins, they demand to have the same rights that are extended to all other Yemenis.

Women in Yemen

According to an old Yemeni proverb, "a girl leaves the house only twice, to her husband and to her grave." Although women have more freedom in modern Yemen than ever before, social and legal traditions still place restrictions on where they can go and what they can do. For instance, women cannot travel, enroll in school, or marry without the permission of their father or their brother. Their access to education is limited, particularly in northern Yemen. As a result, less than half of Yemeni women can read and write.

Women also often have little say in their choice of husband, as their marriages are usually arranged by their parents. Girls can legally be married off at any age. One in four brides is under the age of fifteen. Some are as young as eight. Seeing child brides as an important social problem in Yemeni society, activists are now working to set the legal minimum age for marriage at eighteen.

Arabic is spoken by 221 million people around the world as a first language. Arabic is written using a twenty-eight-letter alphabet. The letters are written and read from right to left. Arabic script is cursive, meaning that each letter is joined to the next. Because the flow of the letters creates beautiful shapes, calligraphy is an important art form throughout the Arabic world.

Classical Arabic is the formal version of the language. It is most often used for reciting passages from the Qur'an. In everyday conversations, Yemenis use a more modern form of Arabic. Several dialects, or local versions, of spoken Arabic are heard in different parts of the country. Because north and south Yemen were politically separate for much of their history, the pronunciation of some words is different in these two regions.

Common Arabic Words and Phrases

Al salaam alaykum	Hello
Ma' al-salama	Good-bye
Tisbah ala-khayr	Good night (to a man)
Tisbihi ala-khayr	Good night (to a woman)
Fursa sa'ida	Pleased to meet you
Kif al-hal?	How are you?
Kif al-'a'ila?	How is your family?
Baraka Allah bik	Thank you
Afwan	You're welcome

A Yemeni man reads about the country's ongoing political crisis in 2015. Dozens of newspapers are published in Yemen.

Only about 70 percent of Yemeni adults are literate, meaning that they can read and write Arabic. Because they have better access to education, the majority of men—about 85 percent—are literate. The literacy rate of women, however, stands at only 55 percent.

Other Languages

Some Yemenis can speak a foreign language. Highly educated Yemenis, for instance, often learn English or French in school. Some older people in the south know Russian because it was the language of the former Soviet Union, with which southern Yemen used to have close political ties. Along the coastal plains, immigrants from Africa speak their own native tongues.

On the island of Socotra, many inhabitants speak Arabic like the Yemenis on the mainland. But among themselves, they sometimes communicate in their own language, called Soqotri. The Soqotri language was never written down until recently. After five years of work, a group of Russian scholars developed a system for writing Soqotri in 2014.

In the al-Mahri governorate in southeastern Yemen, many people speak Mahri, the area's traditional language. Many young people in al-Mahri prefer speaking Arabic, however, leaving older Yemenis there fearing that one day the traditional language will become extinct. Two other languages—Bathari and Hobyot—are even more likely to die out soon. Only a few hundred people in Yemen and neighboring Oman still know these languages.

Somali immigrants walk along a road in southern Yemen. Most Somalis speak the Somali language, and many also speak Arabic.

CHAPTER 8

A Muslim Country

VIRTUALLY EVERYONE IN YEMEN IS A MUSLIM, A follower of Islam. The religion of Islam was introduced to Yemen in 628. At the time, the region was ruled by a Persian governor. After he converted to Islam, he commanded all his subjects to become Muslims as well.

Islam remains the official religion of Yemen. Its tenets are central to the country's legal and political system. The religion also guides Yemenis throughout their lives. Their values and behavior are shaped by their desire to be good Muslims.

Opposite: **Men pray at a mosque in Ibb. When women go to mosques, they pray in a section separate from the men.**

The Prophet

When the people of present-day Yemen first became Muslims, Islam was still a new religion. It began with a prophet named Muhammad. Muhammad was born around 570 in the city of Mecca in what is now Saudi Arabia. Muslims believe that the angel Gabriel began visiting Muhammad when he was about forty years old, delivering messages from God. According to Muslim belief, these messages described God and explained how to worship him properly.

Religions of Yemen (2010 est.)	
Muslim	99%
Sunni	64%
Shi'i	35%
Other	1%
(including Christians, Hindus, Jews, and Baha'is)	

Muhammad's followers compiled the messages into the Qur'an, the holy book of Islam. As more and more people embraced Muhammad's teachings, the authorities in Mecca came to fear that he posed a threat to their political power. Suspecting they were plotting to assassinate him, Muhammad fled Mecca for the city of Medina, also in what is now Saudi Arabia. Muslims call Muhammad's journey to Medina the Hijrah.

The prophet Muhammad died in 632, but Islam continued to attract converts. It eventually spread throughout much of

Girls read the Qur'an at a mosque in Sanaa. Memorizing parts of the Qur'an is considered a virtue.

In the northern city of Sadah, a Shi'i man kisses the tomb of Zayd bin 'Ali, the religious leader who gave the Zaydi sect its name.

Asia and Africa. Islam is now the world's second most common religion, after Christianity. About one out of every four people on earth is Muslim.

Sunnis and Shi'is

Following Muhammad's death, Muslims broke into two main sects—the Sunnis and the Shi'is. The two groups disagreed over who should become the caliph, Muhammad's successor. The Sunnis believed that the new leader should be selected from a group of elites. The Shi'is insisted that the caliph should be a direct descendant of Muhammad.

These divisions within Islam still exist today. Sunnis and Shi'is practice their religion in slightly different ways. About two-thirds of all Yemenis are Sunnis. They primarily live

The call to prayer sounds from minarets such as this one in Sanaa.

in the southwestern region of the country. The other one-third of Yemen's population is Shi'i. Shi'is largely belong to the Zaydi sect, named after Zayd bin 'Ali, a descendant of Muhammad. The Zaydi Shi'is are concentrated in the northern highlands.

The country's recent political upheavals have contributed to religious divisions among the Yemeni people. The Houthi rebels, who took over the capital city of Sanaa in 2014, are Zaydi Shi'is. The regime of President Hadi denounced the power grab and accused the Houthis of wanting to force the Sunni majority to live under Zaydi religious law. The Sunni-Shi'i division has also played a role in determining the allegiances between Yemeni political factions and foreign nations. Iran, whose population is dominated by Shi'i Muslims, has supported the Houthis in the conflict. Saudi Arabia, whose people are primarily Sunni Muslims, began a bombing campaign in Yemen in 2015 in an effort to restore the Hadi government to power.

The Five Pillars

The followers of Islam are supposed to follow a set of specific religious duties. These are called the Five Pillars of Islam.

The first pillar is *shahadah*. It requires Muslims to assert, "There is no god but God and Muhammad is the messenger of God." The second is *salah*. According to this pillar, Muslims must pray five times a day. Mosques, Islamic houses of worship, feature tall towers called minarets. At the appropriate times, the call to prayer is announced from the top of the minaret, signaling to everyone within earshot to stop what they are doing and pray. Traditionally, an official called

A man prays at the Great Mosque in Sanaa.

a *muezzin* ascended to the top of the minaret to give the call to prayer, but today, it is often broadcast from a loudspeaker. When they hear the call to prayer, people kneel facing the holy city of Mecca.

The third pillar of Islam, *zakat*, holds that Muslims give money to the poor. *Sawm*, the fourth pillar, requires them not to eat between sunrise and sunset during Ramadan, the ninth month of the Islamic calendar. The fifth and final pillar is *hajj*. It calls for all Muslims who are physically and financially able to visit Mecca at least once in their lifetime.

Millions of Muslims travel to Mecca every year for the hajj.

Religious Holidays

The longest religious observance each year is Ramadan. Islam holds that it was during this holy month that the angel Gabriel visited Muhammad. Throughout Ramadan, Muslims refrain from eating during daylight hours. They have a meal before dawn and after sunset. The month is a time for spiritual reflection. People make an effort to visit mosques more frequently and read the Qur'an more often.

The end of Ramadan is celebrated with a feast called 'Id al-Fitr. It is a joyous holiday shared with family and friends. People gather together to enjoy all the foods they had denied themselves the previous month. Adults give gifts of candy and money to children, who dress in clothing made just for the holiday.

Another important religious occasion is 'Id al-Adha. The holiday commemorates the sacrifice of the prophet Ibrahim (called Abraham in the Bible) as told in the Qur'an.

A Yemeni family prepares to break their daily fast after sundown during Ramadan.

A Muslim Country **99**

The celebration of 'Id al-Adha includes feasting and dancing. In Yemen, that often means a traditional dance with daggers.

According to the story, Ibrahim proved to God that he was devout by agreeing to kill his son at God's request. God rewarded Ibrahim by sacrificing an animal instead of his son. During 'Id al-Adha, families often kill and cook an animal and host a feast for relatives and friends. Other religious holidays observed by the Yemenis are the birthday of the Prophet Muhammad and the first day of the Islamic calendar.

Non-Muslims

Less than 1 percent of Yemenis are not Muslim. The small number of Christians and Hindus who live there are mostly immigrants from other countries.

Until the mid-twentieth century, there was a vibrant Jewish community in Yemen. Many Yemeni Jews were merchants and craftspeople particularly known for silverwork. But between 1948 and 1950, about fifty thousand Jews left Yemen for the new Jewish state of Israel. The small number of Jews who remain face hostility, particularly from the Houthis, who openly declare their hatred of Jewish people.

A Jewish family relaxes over a meal at their home in Raydah, north of Sanaa. Jewish people have lived in what is now Yemen for at least two thousand years.

CHAPTER 9

A Culture of Old and New

FILLED WITH BEAUTIFUL ARTIFACTS FROM ANCIENT kingdoms, the National Museum of Yemen in Sanaa is a testament to the rich artistic traditions of the country. Art is not a vital part of Yemen's past only. An appreciation of decorative objects, stirring music, and spirited dancing remains central to what it means to be Yemeni today.

Creating Art

In the cities of Yemen, an array of traditional craftwork is for sale at large open-air markets called souqs. Many vendors sell beautiful handmade jewelry, including necklaces, earrings, head ornaments, and nose and finger rings. Many urban Yemenis now prefer gold jewelry, but traditionally, craftspeople made jewelry out of silver. Sometimes they added pieces of coral, amber, or glass for color. The finest silver workers in Yemen were from the

A Yemeni father typically gives his son a jambiya at about age fourteen as a symbol of the transition to adulthood.

Jewish community. Before most of the Yemeni Jews immigrated to Israel, the government made sure that Jewish silver workers passed on their knowledge of the craft so that the Yemeni jewelry making traditions would live on.

Yemeni craftspeople are also known for their *jambiyas*. These decorative J-shaped daggers are ornaments rather than weapons. Men wear them under belts of leather or cloth over their stomachs. The design of a man's jambiya often reflects his status in society. Men of high social rank, for instance, wear jambiyas with silver handles. The most expensive jambiyas have handles made from rhinoceros horns. They take on a glossy sheen as they age.

Today, most cloth used in Yemen is imported from other countries. But some craftspeople still practice the art of weaving. The people of the Tihamah are particularly known for their colorful striped cloth. Along the coastal plains, craftspeople weave palm fronds to make hats and baskets.

For four thousand years, Yemenis have been making *qamarias*. These decorative stained glass windows, often in the shape of a semicircle, adorn many

The Traditional Heritage House

When Arwa Othman was a teenager, she scoured her local marketplace, looking for old handmade objects to buy with her small allowance. Her passion for collecting traditional Yemeni craftwork has continued throughout her life. By 2004, Othman had collected so many objects that she opened her own museum in Sanaa. The Traditional Heritage House exhibited handmade furniture, cookware, leather goods, jewelry, and thousands of books and photographs. Its collection also included 150 traditional costumes from every part of Yemen. Eager to share her fascination with Yemeni culture, Othman welcomed all visitors free of charge.

The Traditional Heritage House, like most museums in Yemen, closed in 2011 because of growing political unrest. But Othman, who was named Yemen's Minister of Culture in 2014, hopes one day to reopen it. "This museum does not belong to me only," she has explained. "It belongs to all Yemenis."

traditional buildings in Yemen. Qamarias are also popular souvenirs purchased by foreign tourists.

Yemen is also home to artists working with more modern media, including painters, sculptors, and photographers. But these artists often have difficulty selling their wares. Many Yemenis, especially religiously conservative people, disapprove of this type of artwork. They believe that creating images by these means is a violation of Islamic law. Largely because of such views, art is rarely taught in Yemeni schools.

Poetry and Literature

Poetry has always been an important part of Yemeni culture. Traditionally, poetry was not written down, but instead committed to memory and recited. Even today, people entertain one another by reciting poems during social gatherings. Often at weddings, men will face off in poetry competitions. Each challenger tries to show off his wit by coming up with the cleverest lines on the spot. In the central highlands, poetry at weddings sometimes takes the form of a performance called the *balah*. Two lines of dancers repeat the lines of a poem made up by one of the participants. They then dance to a drumbeat as the poet thinks up the next verse.

Some poets are famed throughout Yemen. One of the most famous was Abdullah al-Baradouni. The author of twelve books of poetry, he was an outspoken critic of the imams who once ruled northern Yemen. He was imprisoned several times for his political views. Al-Baradouni, who died in 1999, was also an ardent promoter of democratic reform and women's rights. He has been called one of the greatest Arab literary figures of the twentieth century.

Zayd Mutee' Dammaj was another renowned Yemeni writer. This novelist's best-known work is *The Hostage*. It tells the story of a boy taken hostage to make sure his father remains loyal to the government. The book has been translated into many foreign languages. In 2010, the Arab Writers Union placed *The Hostage* in the forty-fifth slot of its ranking of the best one hundred Arabic books ever written.

Making Music

The Yemenis' passion for poetry is almost matched by their love of music. Traditionally, Yemenis have used song to tell romantic stories, to celebrate Allah, and to explore political issues of the day. Often, traditional songs are played on the *oud*, a pear-shaped stringed instrument that is played much like a guitar. Other popular instruments are the *simsimiyya*, a type of lyre, and the *mizmar*, a windpipe.

Some Yemeni singers, such as Abu Bakr Salem and Badavi Zubayr, have become successful recording artists, with fan bases that stretch across the Arab world. But in Yemen, even less-noted singers can make a living performing songs at weddings. Increasingly, though, marrying couples are choosing to play recordings, often by foreign artists, at their wedding celebrations. Even though few can understand the words, guests dance to songs sung in Spanish, French, Indian, and Chinese.

A man strums an oud at his music shop in Sanaa. The oud has been played for more than five thousand years.

The Song of Sanaa

In 2003, the Song of Sanaa was honored by UNESCO as a Masterpiece of the World, a vital practice that helps express the world's cultural diversity. It is not a single song, but a musical style that dates from the fourteenth century. The music is performed by a soloist, who plays a stringed instrument as he sings. Sometimes, he is accompanied by another musician playing an instrument made from a copper plate. Traditionally, the Song of Sanaa was enjoyed during nighttime wedding celebrations and afternoon khat parties.

Ayoob Tarish

One of Yemen's best-loved musicians is Ayoob Tarish, the foremost master of a traditional stringed instrument called the oud. Born in 1942, Tarish began playing music when he was a boy. While his family's herd of goats was grazing, he played on a copper flute tunes he had heard on the radio. After taking up the oud, he began playing songs he wrote for friends and coworkers. Tarish started his professional career as a performer at weddings.

He became a popular performer, and the government asked him to compose the music to the national anthem, "United Republic." His fame was secured after he performed "United Republic" on television. Tarish's career has spanned decades, and he remains beloved today among Yemenis.

A few of the English-language singers enjoyed in Yemen are Celine Dion, Beyoncé, and Shakira.

In recent years, many young Yemenis have embraced rap and hip-hop. The trend began in the 1990s, when Yemeni-American Hajaj Abdulqawi Masaed started combining traditional pipe and lute music with rap lyrics. His single "Yemen: My Great Nation" found an enthusiastic audience in both the United States and Yemen. Yemeni rap artists have since followed his lead, often using their lyrics to share their thoughts on political and social issues.

A Love of Dance

Yemenis love to dance at social events. Dancing styles vary from place to place, with each community having its own favorites. Some dances are very lively, full of skipping and jumping. Dancers on the coastal plain are especially animated. They often perform acrobatic feats or juggle objects—even knives—as part of a dance. Other dances are slow and smooth. During the bird dance, for instance, men move the wide sleeves of their robes to mimic the fluttering of wings.

Yemeni music often includes drums.

Dancing is so important to the Yemenis that they refused to give it up when it was outlawed. From 1914 to 1948, the imam ruling northern Yemen banned singing and dancing, claiming that Islam forbade it. The Yemenis ignored the ban, crowding into underground rooms so they could dance without being seen by the authorities. During this period, musicians invented a small version of the oud that they could hide easily under their clothing.

Playing Sports

The most popular sport in Yemen is soccer. Throughout the country, boys come together on empty lots or fields to play the game, sometimes kicking around a ball of rags if they do not

Camel Jumping

Along the Tihamah region on the coast of the Red Sea, men of the Zaraniq group play a unique sport—camel jumping. The game begins with players taking turns running toward a camel and jumping up and over its back. Everyone who makes the jump successfully continues to the next round, in which another camel is placed next to the first one. The winner is the player who jumps over the greatest number of camels.

have a soccer ball on hand. Yemenis also gather at the Althawra Sports City Stadium in Sanaa to cheer on their national soccer team. Yemen has a national basketball team as well. It competes as a member of the International Basketball Federation.

A more traditional sport enjoyed by Yemenis is camel racing. In the desert, people breed camels that can run quickly through the sand.

Boys play soccer on a beach in Aden.

Nashwan al-Harazi

At twenty-one, Nashwan al-Harazi became the first Yemeni gymnast to compete in the Olympics. When he was a boy, the sport of gymnastics was virtually unknown in Yemen. In a dark, dank gym in Sanaa, he began his training using fifty-year-old equipment. Al-Harazi received some needed inspiration when American coach Jim Holt visited the gym in 1996 as part of the Olympic Solidarity Initiative. Impressed by al-Harazi's determination, Holt pointed at him and told his teammates, "This is him. This could be your guy to compete in the Olympics." Al-Harazi later trained with Holt in Seattle, Washington.

In 2006 and 2007, al-Harazi qualified to compete in the World Gymnastics Championships. The next year, the International Olympic Committee awarded him a wild card spot at the 2008 Summer Olympics in Beijing, China. Al-Harazi competed in three events—floor exercise, vault, and pommel horse. He has since participated in international competitions, while working to develop the sport of gymnastics in his native country.

In the mountains, locals and tourists alike enjoy hiking, skiing, and mountain climbing. The beaches of the coastal plain are excellent for swimming, snorkeling, and scuba diving. The waters off the island of Socotra offer one of the region's best destinations for surfing.

Since 1992, Yemen has sent athletes to every Summer Olympic Games. They have competed in a variety of sports, including gymnastics, swimming, and judo. No Yemeni athlete, however, has ever won an Olympic medal.

CHAPTER 10

Yemeni Ways

S INCE 2015, THE CIVIL WAR HAS DISRUPTED EVERYDAY life in Yemen. The daily routines of Yemenis disappeared as the country became a battlefield with competing interests fighting for control. The war forced civilians to focus all their energy on finding enough food to survive and keeping their loved ones safe.

When at peace, however, Yemenis live very differently. Even though many are poor, they find joy in the close company of their family. The Yemenis also treasure social gatherings, where they chat with their friends and enjoy a shared love of poetry and song.

Food and Drink

The people of Yemen enjoy simple but flavorful food. Their meals often include stews, vegetables, grains, and rice. Wealthy Yemenis might add beef, chicken, or mutton, but most people cannot afford to eat meat on a regular basis. Along the coast, freshly caught fish cooked in a clay oven is a favorite. Nearly all Yemenis avoid pork because Islam forbids eating it.

Opposite: **A boy holds his little sister in the mountains of northern Yemen.**

A woman carries large flatbreads on her head through a market in Sanaa.

At almost every meal, Yemenis eat warm bread with butter. For dessert, they often indulge in *bint al-sahn*, a sweet bread dipped in honey.

In the cities of Yemen, *saltah* is the most popular dish. It is a stew made from chickpeas, lentils, potatoes, spices, and, sometimes, meat, that is served with bread or over rice. Another culinary treat in Yemen is *shafut*, a soup made from sour milk and beans that is poured over bread.

Traditionally, the finest coffee in the world came from Yemen. But few people there drink coffee because it is too expensive. Most Yemenis instead drink *qishr*, a weak brew made from ground coffee husks and flavored with spices and sugar. It is also common to end a meal with sweet, spiced tea.

In most Yemeni households, men eat first. Women and children have their meals later in another room. The food is placed in large bowls or pots on a cloth on the floor. Sitting around the cloth, everyone eats out of the same bowls, using their right hand or a piece of bread to scoop up a bite.

Yemeni Milk Tea

Yemenis and other people in the Gulf region enjoy drinking sweet tea flavored with milk and spices. It is so sweet that some people from other areas think it tastes like a dessert. You can use more or less sugar, depending on how much of a sweet tooth you have. Have an adult help you with this recipe.

Ingredients

2 cups of water

2 tea bags with black tea

4 teaspoons sugar

¼ teaspoon ground cardamom*

¼ teaspoon ground cinnamon

¼ teaspoon ground nutmeg

¼ teaspoon ground cloves

4 ounces evaporated milk (unsweetened)

Directions

1. Pour the water into a small saucepan. Bring it to a boil over medium heat.

2. Cut the strings off the tea bags and add the tea bags to the water. Boil for 3 to 5 minutes.

3. Add the sugar and spices and stir. Turn the heat to low, and simmer for about 10 minutes.

4. Add the milk, and simmer for 2 minutes, stirring occasionally to keep the milk from burning.

5. Carefully remove and discard the tea bags. Pour the tea into two mugs, and serve it with cookies.

*If you do not have all these spices on hand, you can use just two or three of those listed. Just make sure to add a total of two teaspoons of spice.

Many Yemeni men wear both thawbs and Western-style jackets.

Clothing Styles

Men in Yemen often dress in a full-length white gown called a *thawb*, sometimes combining the garment with a black or dark blue jacket. In the coastal regions, men more commonly wear a wraparound skirt called a *futa*, along with a shirt. Men also wear turbans. The way this cloth is tied around their heads indicates where they come from. The look of the jambiya (decorative dagger) they belt to their waist also suggests their status and background.

Islam requires people to dress modestly. When most Yemeni women leave the house, they wear a *niqab*—a black gown that covers them from head to toe except for a narrow eye slit. Many women embrace this tradition, but others wear the niqab because they are afraid of being harassed on the street if they do not. Some younger, less conservative women choose not to cover their faces, though they usually still cover their heads with a *hijab*, or headscarf. Fashionable women like to wear headscarves in bright colors or patterns.

Older women in Sanaa often wear a *sitara*. The sitara is a large piece of cloth they wrap around their bodies. In the past, the pattern on the cloth was colored black, red, and white. More recently, as Yemen began importing more cloth from India, women have taken to wearing sitaras in other colors, including green, blue, and yellow.

Some men and women in cities have embraced Western dress. Men might wear business suits at work. Women might wear jeans under their niqab.

Some Yemeni women wear colorful headscarves, while others cover themselves completely in black.

Housing

The type of house Yemenis have depends on where they live and how much income they have. Because most Yemenis are poor, they typically have small dwellings. In the humid coastal plains, people live in huts made of straw and mud. In the highlands, they live in modest houses constructed from stone or bricks. In the cities, Yemenis might have an apartment, although the poorest people usually call a tent their home.

The housing style most associated with Yemen is the tower house. Sanaa alone has fourteen thousand of them. Today, only fairly wealthy families can afford to live in a tower house.

In the Tihamah region, people sometimes build homes using the trunks of palm trees.

Beautiful tower houses line the narrow streets of Sanaa.

Tower houses are several stories high. The foundation is made from stone. Some houses still standing today have foundations that were first built more than one thousand years ago. The upper levels are made from mud bricks, which are washed with lime to keep out moisture.

The ground floor of a tower house is for storage. The first floor is for entertaining visitors, while the second is for the use of children and women. On the next few floors, there are bedrooms, bathrooms, and the kitchen, topped by an attic. At the very top of the tower house is the *mafraj*, or "room with a view." People use this room to host khat parties and other gatherings.

In the Family

Yemenis are devoted to their families. Several generations of relatives usually share the same household. Grandparents and other older people are treated with respect. They are considered wise, so when there is a dispute within the family, they are often called on to solve it.

Traditionally, a father makes decisions for his wife and children, who are expected to obey him. He also represents the family in most dealings outside the home, including shopping at the souq for food and other necessities. The mother generally stays close to home, where she cooks, cleans, and raises children. In recent years, the rules of what men do and what women do have become less rigid. For instance, many women, especially younger ones, now work at jobs outside the home.

Paying for a Wedding

In Yemen, the cost of marrying is high. The groom is expected to pay for the wedding ceremony, the couple's new home and furnishing, and clothing and gifts for his bride. With a high rate of unemployment, many young men cannot save enough money to marry. In rural areas, they rely on *al-jibaya* (financial support), an old tradition dating back to the tenth century. At the end of a wedding, a scarf is placed on the floor. The guests toss money into the scarf as an announcer tells the crowd the amount donated to the groom. Some Yemenis are critical of the tradition, because guests will often compete to offer the biggest gifts, sometimes even going into debt to do so.

The tradition of al-jibaya has largely died out in Yemen's cities. And there, some brides who work outside the home are bucking tradition by contributing to the marriage costs. Often, though, women have to keep their contributions secret so that their more conservative relatives do not think less of their husbands-to-be.

A Yemeni girl gives her sister a ride on a wheelbarrow. About two-thirds of Yemen's population is under age twenty-five.

Generally, boys are given greater freedom than girls. They are allowed to wander outside and play with their friends. Girls often have to stay indoors and look after their younger siblings. In rural areas, children are put to work in the fields. They also help tend their family's herds of animals.

All children are required to go to primary school from the ages of six to fifteen. Some continue on to secondary school until they are eighteen. Families living outside cities are less

Many young Yemenis work to help their families survive. The Mobile School initiative travels to where children live, providing education to those who are not able to attend school regularly.

likely to send their children to school. The school might be far away, making getting there too difficult, or the children's labor might be needed on the family farm. As a result, only about 72 percent of Yemeni children get a primary school education.

Social Life

Yemenis place a high value on hospitality. They always offer food to guests in their home. Guests cannot refuse the food, or they risk insulting their hosts.

Whether at the souq or on the street, Yemenis make time to chat with any friends and neighbors they come upon. In the afternoon, they might stop working to sip tea and catch up with friends. Public bathhouses are also sites for casual get-togethers. Anyone can go to a bathhouse, but men and women are admitted on different days.

Generally, women and men do not socialize with each other. But recently, many Internet cafés have opened in Yemeni cities. These popular spots are the only places where it is socially acceptable for a man and a woman to share a table, a snack, and a conversation.

Yemenis often gather to watch television together. Watching television is usually a family activity, but friends might stop by

Yemeni schoolgirls relax during recess.

to see a favorite show. The government operates two television stations, and Yemenis also watch programs broadcast from Saudi Arabia and Oman. Shows include sports programs, comedies, and soap operas. Television news plays a particularly important role in Yemen. Because so much of the population is unable to read, many Yemenis rely on television news, rather than newspapers, to find out about current events.

The social event most associated with Yemen is the khat party. Every afternoon, Yemenis get together with friends to chew khat leaves. Chewing khat releases a mild stimulant that makes people feel energetic. During a khat party, friends chat, joke,

Boys gather around a television on a street in Sanaa. Few families in Yemen have their own TV.

recite poetry, and discuss politics and other serious issues. People often chew khat during business meetings because they believe it can clear their minds and help them make better decisions. Students chew khat because they think it helps them study.

Dominoes is a popular pastime in Yemeni cafés.

Celebrating Yemen's Past

Every year, Yemenis commemorate important events in their country's history. For instance, September 26 is known as Revolution Day. It honors the day the military overthrew the ruling imam in northern Yemen in 1962. November 30 is called Independence Day. This holiday celebrates the day the people of southern Yemen revolted against British rule in 1967.

The most important national holiday in Yemen is National Unity Day, which commemorates the unification of northern and southern Yemen in 1990. Schoolchildren march through the streets, waving Yemen's flag and singing "United Republic," the

Public Holidays

January 1	New Year's Day
May 1	Labor Day
May 22	National Unity Day
September 26	Revolution Day
October 14	National Day
November 30	Independence Day

Girls perform at an event commemorating Revolution Day.

national anthem. Yemenis celebrate publicly with parades and dancing and privately with family gatherings in their home. With relatives and friends, many huddle around the television to hear the president's Unity Day speech.

In 2014, President Hadi used the occasion to encourage his people to embrace the governmental reforms outlined when the new constitution was written after Saleh left office. He assured that the new national government would represent everyone in Yemen. The process of reform "excludes no one," Hadi promised. "The door is still open."

The following year, there was no National Unity Day celebration. Hadi was living in exile in Saudi Arabia, and the nation had broken into warring factions, each with a different vision for Yemen. As they battled for control, the future of Yemen itself became uncertain. The only thing clear was the hard road ahead for the Yemeni people who, when the fighting stops, will face the daunting task of rebuilding their lives and their society amid the rubble left behind.

Children in Sanaa scramble over the rubble of a building destroyed in a Saudi air strike.

Timeline

YEMENI HISTORY

A series of ancient kingdoms begin ruling southern Arabia.	**ca. 1200 BCE**
The Marib Dam breaks, leading to the end of the Saba kingdom.	**500s CE**
Islam is introduced to southern Arabia.	**628**
Imams of the Zaydi Shi'i sect of Islam begin ruling northern Yemen.	**ca. 890**
Queen Arwa rules in southern Arabia.	**Late 1000s**
Turks of the Ottoman Empire occupy much of Yemen.	**1530s–1540s**
The Zaydis seize control of northern Yemen from the Ottoman Turks.	**1630s**
The British take over the port city of Aden.	**1839**
The Ottoman Turks and the British establish a border between North and South Yemen.	**1905**
The Turks withdraw from North Yemen.	**1918**

WORLD HISTORY

ca. 2500 BCE	The Egyptians build the pyramids and the Sphinx in Giza.
ca. 563 BCE	The Buddha is born in India.
313 CE	The Roman emperor Constantine legalizes Christianity.
610	The Prophet Muhammad begins preaching a new religion called Islam.
1054	The Eastern (Orthodox) and Western (Roman Catholic) Churches break apart.
1095	The Crusades begin.
1215	King John seals the Magna Carta.
1300s	The Renaissance begins in Italy.
1347	The plague sweeps through Europe.
1453	Ottoman Turks capture Constantinople, conquering the Byzantine Empire.
1492	Columbus arrives in North America.
1500s	Reformers break away from the Catholic Church, and Protestantism is born.
1776	The U.S. Declaration of Independence is signed.
1789	The French Revolution begins.
1865	The American Civil War ends.
1879	The first practical lightbulb is invented.
1914	World War I begins.
1917	The Bolshevik Revolution brings communism to Russia.

YEMENI HISTORY

The Yemen Arab Republic is established.	**1962**
The People's Republic of South Yemen (later renamed the People's Democratic Republic of Yemen) is founded.	**1967**
Ali Abdullah Saleh becomes the president of the Yemen Arab Republic.	**1978**
Oil is discovered in Yemen.	**1980s**
The two Yemens unite to form the Republic of Yemen; Ali Abdullah Saleh becomes the country's president.	**1990**
The Republic of Yemen adopts a constitution; as many as one million Yemeni workers are expelled from Saudi Arabia.	**1991**
Civil war breaks out in Yemen; Saleh puts down the revolt of southern secessionists.	**1994**
Al-Qaeda terrorists bomb the USS *Cole* in the port of Aden.	**2000**
Anti-government protesters in Tahrir Square demand an end to the Saleh regime; Yemeni activist Tawakkol Karman wins the Nobel Peace Prize; Saleh resigns.	**2011**
Abdu Rabbu Mansour Hadi is elected president of Yemen.	**2012**
Houthi rebels take over the capital city of Sanaa.	**2014**
Hadi escapes to Saudi Arabia; Saudi Arabia begins a bombing campaign against Houthi forces.	**2015**

WORLD HISTORY

1929	A worldwide economic depression begins.
1939	World War II begins.
1945	World War II ends.
1969	Humans land on the Moon.
1975	The Vietnam War ends.
1989	The Berlin Wall is torn down as communism crumbles in Eastern Europe.
1991	The Soviet Union breaks into separate states.
2001	Terrorists attack the World Trade Center in New York City and the Pentagon near Washington, D.C.
2004	A tsunami in the Indian Ocean destroys coastlines in Africa, India, and Southeast Asia.
2008	The United States elects its first African American president.

Fast Facts

Official name: Republic of Yemen

Capital: Sanaa

Official language: Arabic

Sanaa

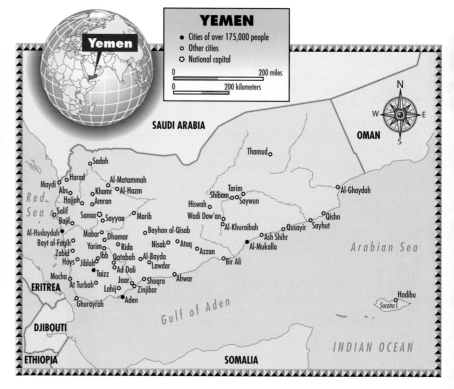

National flag

Stone bridge at Shaharah

Official religion:	Islam
Year of founding:	1990
National anthem:	"United Republic"
Government:	Republic
Head of state:	President
Head of government:	Prime minister
Area of country:	203,850 square miles (527,969 sq km)
Latitude and longitude of geographic center:	15°00' N, 48°00' E
Bordering countries:	Oman to the east, Saudi Arabia to the north
Highest elevation:	12,336 feet (3,760 m) above sea level, at Mount al-Nabi Shu'ayb
Lowest elevation:	Sea level along the coast
Average high temperature:	In Sanaa, 72°F (22°C) in January, 80°F (27°C) in July; in Aden, 82°F (28°C) in January, 97°F (36°C) in July
Average low temperature:	In Sanaa, 37°F (3°C) in January, 56°F (13°C) in July; in Aden, 73°F (23°C) in January, 84°F (29°C) in July
Average annual precipitation:	In Sanaa, 10 inches (25 cm); in Aden, 1.6 inches (4 cm)

Temple of the Moon

National population (July 2014 est.):	26,053,000	
Population of major cities (2010 est.):	Sanaa	2,833,000
	Aden	855,000
	Taizz	467,000
	Al-Hudaydah	410,000
	Al-Mukalla	182,500

Landmarks:
- ▶ *Dar al-Hajar*, Wadi Dhahr
- ▶ *Great Dam of Marib*, Marib
- ▶ *Great Mosque of Sanaa*, Sanaa
- ▶ *Saleh Mosque*, Sanaa
- ▶ *Temple of the Moon*, Marib

Economy: About 65 percent of the government's revenue comes from oil resources, which are almost depleted. Since 2009, Yemen has also exported liquefied natural gas. Major agricultural products include khat, apricots, mangoes, guavas, potatoes, onions, tomatoes, sorghum, wheat, alfalfa, and barley. The nation has a small manufacturing sector, which produces petroleum products, bricks, cement, and metal. Some Yemenis also produce traditional crafts.

Currency

Currency: The rial. In 2015, 10 rials equaled 5 U.S. cents, and US$1 was worth 215 Yemeni rials.

System of weights and measures: Metric system

Literacy rate (2015): 70%

Schoolchildren

Tawakkol Karman

Common Arabic words and phrases:

Al salaam alaykum	Hello
Ma' al-salama	Good-bye
Tisbah ala-khayr	Good night (to a man)
Tisbihi ala-khayr	Good night (to a woman)
Fursa sa'ida	Pleased to meet you
Kif al-hal?	How are you?
Kif al-'a'ila?	How is your family?
Baraka Allah bik	Thank you
Afwan	You're welcome

Prominent Yemenis:

Abdullah al-Baradouni   (1929–1999)
Poet

Arwa   (1045–1138)
Queen in southern Arabia

Bilqis (Queen of Sheba)   (ca. 900s BCE)
Ruler of the kingdom of Saba

Zayd Mutee' Dammaj   (1943–2000)
Novelist

Abdu Rabbu Mansour Hadi   (1945–)
President

Tawakkol Karman   (1979–)
Nobel Peace Prize winner

Ali Abdullah Saleh   (1942–)
Former president

Ayoob Tarish   (1942–)
Singer and musician

To Find Out More

Books

▶ Blashfield, Jean F. *Yemen*. Chicago: Heinemann Library, 2012.

▶ Guillain, Charlotte. *Islamic Culture*. Chicago: Heinemann Library, 2013.

▶ O'Neal, Claire. *We Visit Yemen*. Hockessin, DE: Mitchell Lane Publishers, 2012.

Music

▶ *Qat, Coffee & Qambus; Raw 45s From Yemen*. Atlanta: Dust-to-Digital, 2013.

▶ Salem, Abu Bakr. *Ahtafel Berjarh*. Riyadh, Saudi Arabia: Rotana Records, 2007.

▶ *The Yemen Tihama: Trance & Dance Music From the Red Sea Coast of Arabia*. Uppingham, England: Topic Records, 2002.

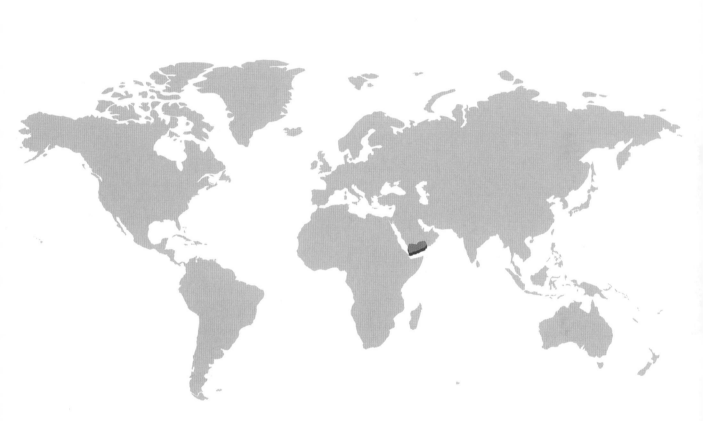

▶ Visit this Scholastic Web site for more information on Yemen:
www.factsfornow.scholastic.com
Enter the keyword Yemen

Index

Page numbers in *italics* indicate illustrations.

A

acacia trees, 33, *33*
Aden. *See also* cities.
　Abdu Rabbu Mansour Hadi in, 62
　air strikes in, 63
　as capital, 23, *53*
　children in, *110*
　climate of, 20
　Crater, 23
　Great Britain in, 47–48, *47*
　population of, 23, 86
　port of, 47, 48, 75–76
　protests in, 13
　Tawila Tanks, 23, *23*
　tourism in, 80
Aden Protectorate, 48
African-Arab people, 85
agriculture
　coastal plains, 24, 32, 76
　coffee, 23, 46, 77
　crops, 23, 27, 29, 77
　date palms, 29, 34
　economy and, 75, 76–78, 79
　employment in, *77*
　farmland, 75, 76
　fruit trees, 29, 33–34
　highlands region, 28
　irrigation, 24, 27, 29, 32, 45, 76, 78
　khat, 23, 27, *27*, 77, 78, *78*

livestock, 26, 35, *40*, 41, 76, *77*, 78, 113
Rub' al-Khali, 26
Sabaean kingdom, 45
social class and, 86
terraces, 29, 34, 76
Tihamah region, 24, 32, 76
wadis, 76
World Bank and, 27
Ahmad (imam), 50–51
al-Ahrar al-Yamaniyyin (Free Yemenis), 49–50
Akhdam ("servants"), 86, 87, *87*
Al-Hudaydah, 23, 86
Al-Mukalla, 86
Althawra Sports City Stadium, 110
animal life
　Arabian leopard, 35, *35*
　Arabian oryx, 41, *41*
　birds, *30*, 35
　camels, 35, 78, 110, *110*
　coastal plains, 32
　conservation, 35, 40
　deserts, 26, 32, *32*
　donkeys, *77*, 78
　Egyptian vultures, *30*
　endangered species, 35, 41, *41*
　extinct species, 41
　hamadryas baboons, 34
　highlands, 33
　livestock, 26, 35, *40*, 41, 76, *77*, 78, 113
　mountains, 34
　Queen of Sheba's gazelle, 41
　Rub' al-Khali, 26
　Socotra Island, 22, 37, 80
　Tihamah region, 32
Arabian leopard (national animal), 35, *35*
Arabian oryx, 41, *41*
Arabian Peninsula, 19
Arabian Sea, 19, 21, 22

Arabic language, 86, 89–90, *89*, 91, *91*
Arab people, 85
Arab Spring, 60, *60*
Arab Writers Union, 106
art, 103–105
Arwa (queen), 46, 133
al-Ashrafiya mosque, 23, *23*
Asian people, 85

B

Bab al-Mandab strait, 21, *21*, 22
al-Badr, Muhammad, 50, 51, *51*, 52
balah (poetry performance), 106
al-Baradouni, Abdullah, 106, 133
Bathari language, 91
bathhouses, 122–123
al-Bayd, Ali Salim, 55
Bedouin people, 26, 86
Ben Ali, Zine El Abidine, 13
Bible, 43, 44, 46, 99–100
Bilqis (Queen of Sheba), 46, 133
bint al-sahn (food), 114
birds, *30*, 35
birth rate, 85
borders, 20, 21, 48, *52*, 54

C

calendar, 98, 101
camels, 35, 78, 110, *110*
capital city. *See* Sanaa.
central highlands, 105–106
Change Square, 13, 14
children, *24*, *36*, *54*, 84, 85, 88, *88*, 94, *110*, *112*, 114, 121, *121*, *122*, *123*, *124*, *127*
Christianity, 34, 43, 44, 46, 93, 95, 99–100
cities. *See also* Aden; Sanaa; villages.
　Al-Hudaydah, 23, 86
　Al-Mukalla, 86
　Ibb, 92
　Jiblah, 46

Sadah, 95
Taizz, 13, 23, *23*, 28, 69, 86
civil war, 51–52, 54, 61, 75, 76, 83, 113
climate, 20, 24, 26, 28, 29
clothing, 9, 105, 116–117, *116*, *117*
coastal plain, *22*, 24–25, *24*, 80, 111
coastline, *24*, 80
coffee, *23*, 46, 77, 114
communications, 8, 12, 13, 55, 90, 124, *124*
communism, 53
constitution, 65, 71, 73
Council of Ministers, 35, 66
crafts, 79, 103–105
Crater, 23
cucumber trees, 37, *37*
currency (rial), 82, *82*

D
daggers. See *jambiyas*.
Dammaj, Zayd Mutee', 106, 133
dams, 45
dancing, *100*, 106, 108–109, 126
Dar al-Hajar, 49, *49*
date palms, 29, 34
desert rose trees, 38, *38*
deserts, 19, 22, 25–26, *26*, 32, *32*, 86
dhows (boats), *24*
Djibouti, 21
dominoes, *125*
donkeys, *77*, 78
dragon's blood (national tree), 39, 40, *40*

E
economy
    Ali Abdullah Saleh and, 54, 59, 82, 83
    agriculture, 75, 76–78, 79
    civil war and, 75, 76, 83
    currency (rial), 82, *82*

employment, 10, 56, *56*, *77*, 79, 120, *122*
exports, 27, 34, 48, 81
fishing industry, 78
foreign aid, 51, 53, 55, 59, 82
geography and, 75
gross domestic product (GDP), *81*
imports, 78
khat and, 78, *78*
manufacturing, 79
mining, 79, 81
oil industry, 19, 76, 81, *81*
People's Democratic Republic of Yemen (PDRY), 55
service industries, 79–80
Soviet Union and, 55
tourism, 22, 23, 39, 46, 58, 80, *80*, 105
trade, 43, *44*, 75–76
unification and, 75, 76
Yemen Arab Republic (YAR), 54
education, 53, 79, 86, 87, 90, 105, 121–122, *122*, *123*, 125
Egypt, 44, 51, 52
Egyptian vultures, *30*
elderly people, 120
elections, 57, *57*, 61, 65
employment, 10, 56, *56*, *77*, 79, 86, 120, *122*
Empty Quarter, 19, 22, 25–26, *26*, 32, *32*
endangered species, 35, 41, *41*
English language, 108
Eritrea, 21
Ethiopian people, 44
executive branch of government, 10, 11, 13, 14, 15, 54–55, *55*, 56, 57, *57*, 59, 60–61, *61*, 61–62, 63, 65–66, 67, 68, *68*, 70, *71*, 73, 82, 83, 96, 127, 133
exports, 27, 34, 48, 81
extinct species, 41

F
families, *84*, *112*, 120, 126–127
Federation of South Arabia, 52
fishing industry, 78
Five Pillars of Islam, 97–98, *98*
foods, 23, 33, 34, *34*, 77, 78, 83, 99, *99*, 100, *101*, 113–114, *114*, 115, *115*
foreign aid, 51, 53, 55, 59, 82, 83
frankincense, 43, 44, 45
fruit trees, 29, 33–34

G
games, *125*
Gbowee, Leymah, 14, *15*
geography
    borders, 20, 21, 48, *52*, 54
    coastal plain, 22, *22*, 24–25, *24*, 80, 111
    deserts, 19, 22, 25–26, *26*
    economy and, 75
    elevation, 20, 28
    highlands region, 22, 28–29, *28*
    islands, 20, 21–22, *22*
    land area, 20, 21
    mountains, 20, 28, 80
    straits, 21, *21*
    volcanoes, 23
    wadis, 20, 29, *29*
government
    Aden Protectorate, 48
    Ali Abdullah Saleh, 10, 11, 13, 14, 54, 55, 56, 57, *57*, 59, 60–61, 61–62, 68, *68*, 70, *70*, *71*, 82, 83, 127, 133
    Abdu Rabbu Mansour Hadi, 15, 61, *61*, 63, 70, *71*, 73, 96, 127, 133
    communications and, 12, 13, 124
    communism and, 53
    conservation and, 35, 40–41
    constitution, 65, 71, 73

Council of Ministers, 35, 66

coups, 50–51, 62, 125

dancing and, 109

elections, 57, *57*, 61, 65

executive branch, 10, 11, 13, 14, 15, 54–55, *55*, 56, 57, *57*, 59, 60–61, *61*, 61–62, 63, 65–66, 67, 68, *68*, 70, *71*, 73, 82, 83, 96, 127, 133

Federation of South Arabia, 52

governorates, 67

Great Britain and, 46, 47–48, *47*, 51, 52, 53

Gulf Cooperation Council (GCC), 60–61, 70

Houthis and, 73, *73*

imams, 45, 46, 48, 49, *49*, 50–51, *50*, 52, 106, 109

independence, 52, 125, 126

Islamic religion and, 66, 93, 96, 105

journalism and, 12, 13

judicial branch, 65, 66, 67

legislative branch, 64, 65, 66, 67

local government, 67–68

military, *47*, 48, 50–51, 62, 63, *63*, 125

Minister of Culture, 105

National Liberation Front, 52

oil industry and, 81

Ottoman Empire and, 46, 48

People's Democratic Republic of Yemen (PDRY), 23, 52–54, *55*, 75

People's Republic of Yemen, 11

political parties, 13, 71

prime ministers, 65–66

protests, *12*, 13–14, *16*, 60, *60*, *63*, 70, 82–83, 87

Republic of Yemen, 11, 17, 55, 66

Revolutionary Committee, 73

Sanaa and, 72

Saudi Arabia and, 51

sheikhs, 16

Supreme Court, 66

term limits, 65, 66, 71

unification, 11, 54, 55, *55*, 66, 75, 76, 125–126

Yemen Arab Republic (YAR), 11, 51, 54

Great Britain, 46, 47–48, *47*, 51, 52, 53, 125

Great Mosque, 72, 97

gross domestic product (GDP), *81*

Gulf Cooperation Council (GCC), 60–61, 70

Gulf of Aden, 21, 23

H

Hadi, Abdu Rabbu Mansour
   in Aden, 62
   election of, 61, 73
   escape of, 62, 63, 127
   Houthis and, 62, 96
   inauguration of, 15, *71*
   presidency of, 15, 61, 62, 70, *71*, 73, 96, 133
   al-Qaeda and, 15
   resignation of, 62
   Saudi Arabia and, 62, 63, 96, 127
   Unity Day speech, 127
   as vice president, 61, *61*, 70

hajj (Fifth Pillar of Islam), 98, *98*

hamadryas baboons, 54

Hanish Island, 22

al-Harazi, Nashwan, 111, *111*

health care, 40, 83, 85, 87

highlands region, 22, 28–29, *28*, 33

hijab (clothing), 117, *117*

hip-hop music, 108

historical maps. *See also* maps.
   Colonial Yemen (1904), *48*
   Divided Yemen (1967–1990), *52*
   Early Trade Routes, *44*

Hobyot language, 91

holidays
   national, 125–127, *126*
   religious, 99–100, *99*, *100*, 101

Holt, Jim, 111

honey, 34, *34*

hospitality, 122

House of Representatives, 64

housing, 41, 87, *101*, 118–120, *118*, *119*

al-Houthi, Mohammed Ali, 73, *73*

Houthi people, 16–17, *16*, 57, 62–63, *63*, 73, *73*, 96, 101

I

Ibb, 92

Ibrahim (prophet), 99–100

'Id al-Adha holiday, 99–100, *100*

'Id al-Fitr holiday, 99

imams, 45, 46, 48, 49, *49*, 50–51, *50*, 52, 106, 109

immigration, 100

imports, 78

independence, 52, 125, 126

Independence Day, 125, 126

insect life, 32, 35–36

International Basketball Federation, 110

International Monetary Fund, 82

Internet, 13, 123

Iran, 44, 63, 96

Iraq, 56

irrigation, 24, 27, 29, 32, 45, 76, 78

Islah (political party), 13

Islamic religion. *See also* religion.
   art and, 105
   calendar, 98, 101
   caliphs, 95
   clothing and, 116–117
   dancing and, 109
   fasting, 99
   Five Pillars of Islam, 97–98, *98*

foods and, 113
government and, 66, 93, 96, 105
holidays, 99–100, 99, 100, 101
Houthis and, 16, 57, 96
Ibrahim (prophet), 99–100
'Id al-Adha holiday, 99–100, 100
'Id al-Fitr holiday, 99
judicial branch of government
    and, 66
minarets, 97–98, 96
mosques, 23, 58, 58, 72, 92, 94, 96,
    97, 97
muezzin (Muslim official), 97–98
Muhammad (Islamic prophet), 16,
    44–45, 93–94, 95, 96, 99, 100
Nobel Peace Prize and, 14
Persians and, 44
prayer, 92, 96, 97–98, 97
prevalence of, 93, 94–95
Qur'an, 43, 46, 89, 94, 94, 99–100
Ramadan (holy month), 98, 99,
    99, 101
sharia law, 66, 105
Shi'i Muslims, 45, 57, 93, 95–96,
    95
spread of, 94–95
Sunni Muslims, 93, 95–96
women and, 92, 94, 94
Zaydi sect, 95, 96
Israel, 52, 101

J
jambiyas (daggers), 79, 104, 104, 116
Jesus, 34, 44
jewelry, 103–104
al-jibaya (marriage tradition), 120
Jiblah, 46
Judaism, 100–101, 101
judicial branch of government, 65,
    66, 67

K
Kamaran Island, 22
Karman, Tawakkol, 8, 9–10, 11,
    12–13, 14, 15, 17, 46, 133
khat, 23, 27, 27, 77, 78, 78, 120,
    124–125
Kuwait, 56

L
languages, 86, 89–90, 89, 90–91, 91,
    107–108
legislative branch of government, 64,
    65, 66, 67
literacy rate, 53, 90, 124
literature, 106, 133
livestock, 26, 35, 40, 41, 76, 77, 78,
    113
local government, 67–68
locusts, 36

M
mafraj ("room with a view"), 120
al-Mahri governorate, 91
Mahri language, 91
manufacturing, 79
maps. *See also* historical maps.
    geopolitical, 10
    population density, 86
    resources, 76
    Sanaa, 72
    topographical, 20
Marib Dam, 45
Marib Reservoir, 20
marine life, 23, 78, 80, 113
marriage, 88, 105, 106, 107, 108, 120
Masaed, Hajaj Abdulqawi, 108
Masterpiece of the World, 107
Mecca, Saudi Arabia, 93, 98, 98
Medina, Saudi Arabia, 94
military, 47, 48, 50–51, 62, 63, 63,
    125
milk tea, 115, 115

minarets, 96, 97–98
mining, 79, 81
Minister of Culture, 105
mizmar (musical instrument), 106
Mobile School initiative, 122
Mount al-Nabi Shu'ayb, 20, 28
Mount Bura, 80
Mount Sabr, 23
muezzin (Muslim official), 97–98
al-Muhamasheen ("marginalized
    people"), 87, 87
Muhammad (Islamic prophet), 16,
    44–45, 93–94, 95, 96, 99, 100
music, 69, 106–108, 107, 108, 109,
    113, 133
myrrh, 43, 44, 45

N
national anthem, 69, 108, 126
National Day, 126
national flag, 66, 66, 71
national holidays, 125–127, 126
national language, 86
National Liberation Front, 52
National Museum of Yemen, 103
national religion, 93
National Unity Day, 125–127
natural gas, 81
newspapers, 55, 90, 124
niqab (clothing), 9, 116–117
Nobel Peace Prize, 14, 15, 46, 133
nomads, 26, 35
Noman, Abdullah Abdulwahab, 69
North Yemen, 45, 46, 48, 50, 51, 57,
    66, 68, 75, 89, 106, 109, 125, 126

O
oil industry, 19, 76, 81, 81
Olympic Games, 111, 111
Oman, 21, 91, 124
Othman, Arwa, 105
Ottoman Empire, 46, 48

oud (musical instrument), 106, *107*, 108, 109

P

people. *See also* women.
  African-Arabs, 85
  Akhdam ("servants"), 86, 87, *87*
  Arabs, 85
  Asians, 85
  Bedouins, 26, 86
  birth rate, 85
  children, *24*, *36*, *54*, 84, 85, 88, *88*, *94*, *110*, *112*, 114, 121, *121*, *122*, *123*, *124*, *127*
  clothing, 9, 105, 116–117, *116*, *117*
  early kingdoms, 43
  education, 53, 79, 86, 87, 90, 105, 121–122, *122*, *123*, 125
  elderly, 120
  employment, 10, 56, *56*, *77*, 79, 86, 120, *122*
  Ethiopians, 44
  families, *84*, *112*, 120, 126–127
  foods, 23, 33, 34, *34*, 77, 78, 83, 99, 100, *101*, 113–114, *114*, 115, *115*
  health care, 40, 83, 85, 87
  hospitality, 122
  housing, 41, 87, *101*, 118–120, *118*, *119*
  Houthis, 16–17, *16*, 57, 62–63, *63*, 73, *73*, 96, 101
  immigration, 100
  infant mortality, 87
  jambiyas (daggers) and, 104, 116
  languages, 86, 89–90, 89, 90–91, *91*, 107–108
  life expectancy, 85
  literacy rate, 53, 90, 124
  marriage, 88, 105, 106, 107, 108, 120

nomads, 26, 35
Persians, 44–45
population, 23, 27, 86, 86
poverty, 10, 11, *11*, 58, 75, 76, 87, 87, 113
Sabaeans, *42*, 43, 45, *45*
socialization, 78, *78*, 105, 109, 122–125, *125*
social rank, 86, 104, 116
Somali, *91*
Turks, 46
Zaraniq, 110, *110*
Zaydi sect, 45, 46, 48, 51, 57, *95*, 96
People's Democratic Republic of Yemen (PDRY), 23, 52–54, *54*, 55, 69, 75
People's Mosque, 58, *58*
People's Republic of Yemen, 11
Perim Island, 22
Persian people, 44–45
plant life
  acacia trees, 33, *33*
  coastal plain, 32
  conservation, 40
  cucumber trees, 37, *37*
  date palms, 29, 34
  desert rose trees, 38, *38*
  deserts, 26, 32
  dragon's blood trees, 39, 40, *40*
  fruit trees, 29, 33–34
  highlands region, 28, 33
  khat, 23, 27, *27*, 77, 78, *78*, 120, 124–125
  Rub' al-Khali, 26, 32
  Sidr tree, 34
  Socotra Island, 22, 37–38, 80
  Tihamah region, 32
  tourism and, 39
poetry, 105–106, 113, 133
political parties, 13, 71
population, 23, 27, 86, 86

poverty, 10, 11, *11*, 58, 75, 76, 87, *87*, 113
presidents. *See* Hadi, Abdu Rabbu Mansour; Saleh, Ali Abdullah.
prime ministers, 65–66
protests, *12*, 13–14, *16*, 60, *60*, 63, 70, 82–83, 87

Q

al-Qaeda terrorist network, 15, 27, 57, 59
qamarias (stained-glass windows), 104–105
al-Qasim ar-Rassi, Yahya bin al-Husayn bin, 45
qishr (beverage), 114
Queen of Sheba. *See* Bilqis.
Queen of Sheba's gazelle, 41
Qur'an (Islamic holy book), 43, 46, 89, 94, *94*, 99–100

R

Ramadan (Islamic holy month), 98, 99, *99*, 101
rap music, 108
recipe, 115, *115*
Red Sea, 19, 21, 22, 28
religion. *See also* Islamic religion.
  Abraham, 99–100
  Bible, 43, 44, 46, 99–100
  Christianity, 34, 43, 44, 46, 93, 95, 99–100
  Jesus, 34, 44
  Judaism, 100–101, *101*
reptilian life, 35, 36, *36*, 39, *39*
Republic of Yemen, 11, 17, 55, 66
Revolutionary Committee, 73
Revolution Day, 125, *126*
rial (currency), 82, *82*
Rock Palace, 49, *49*
Roman Empire, 43
Rub' al-Khali, 25–26, *26*, 32

Russian language, 90

S

Sadah, 95
Sabaean kingdom, *42*, 43, 45, *45*
salah (Second Pillar of Islam), 97–98
Saleh, Ali Abdullah
    corruption of, 59, 70, 82
    economy and, 54, 59, 82, 83
    election of, 57, *57*
    Houthis and, 16, 62
    Islah party and, 13
    journalism and, 12
    presidency of, 11, 14, 54, 55, *55*,
        61–62, 68, *68*, 133
    protests against, 10, 13–14, 60,
        70, *70*
    al-Qaeda and, 59, 60
    Republic of Yemen and, 11
    resignation of, 14, 60–61, *71*
    Saleh Mosque and, 58
    secessionists and, 56
    unification and, 55, *55*
    Yemen Arab Republic (YAR) and,
        11, 54
Saleh Mosque, 58, *58*, 82
Salem, Abu Bakr, 107
al-Sallal, Abdullah, 51, 52
saltah (food), 114
Sanaa. *See also* cities.
    age of, 72
    air strikes in, *127*
    Akhdam ("servants") in, 87
    Althawra Sports City Stadium,
        110
    architecture in, 72, *72*
    children in, *124*
    climate, 20, *25*
    clothing in, 117
    Dar al-Hajar, 49, *49*
    employment in, 86
    foods in, *114*

founding of, 31
government in, 72
Great Mosque, 72, *97*
House of Representatives, *64*
housing in, 118–120, *119*
Houthis in, *16*, 62, 96
map of, *72*
mosques in, 13, 58, *58*, 72, 82, *94*,
    96, 97
music in, 107, *107*
National Museum of Yemen, 103
population of, 23, 72, 86
protests in, *12*, 13–14, 60, *60*, 70
Saleh Mosque, 58, *58*
sandstorms in, *25*
Song of Sanaa, 107
souqs in, 72, *102*
Tahrir Square, 9, 10, *12*, 13, 60, *60*
tourism in, 80
tower houses, 118–120, *119*
Traditional Heritage House, 105
women in, *83*
sandstorms, 25, *25*
Saudi Arabia, 17, 20, 21, 48, 50, 51,
    56, 57, 62, 63, 81, 93, 94, 96, 98,
    98, 124, *127*
sawm (Fourth Pillar of Islam), 98
scorpions, 32, *32*
secessionist movement, 56, 57, 62
service industries, 79–80
shahadah (First Pillar of Islam), 97
Shaharah, 18
sharia law, 66, 105
sheikhs, 16
Shi'i Muslims, 45, 57, 93, 95–96, *95*
Sidr tree, 34
silver workers, 103–104
simsimiyya (musical instrument), 106
Sirleaf, Ellen Johnson, 14
sitara (clothing), 117
soccer, 109–110, *110*

socialization, 78, *78*, 105, 109, 122–
    125, *125*
social rank, 86, 104, 116
Socotra Island, 20, 22, *22*, 37–39, *39*,
    40–41, 80, 84, 91
Socotran chameleons, 39, *39*
Solomon, king of Israel, 46
Somali language, *91*
Somali people, *91*
Song of Sanaa, 107
Soqotri language, 91
Souq al-Milh, 72
souqs, 72, *102*, 103, 120, 122
South Yemen, 46, 47, 48, 52, 53, *53*,
    66, 75, 89, 126
Soviet Union, 51, 53, *54*, 55, 76,
    90–91
sports, 109–110, *110*, 111, *111*, 124
Sunni Muslims, 93, 95–96
Supreme Court, 66

T

Tahrir Square, 9, 10, *12*, 13, 60, *60*
Taizz, 13, 23, *23*, 28, 69, 86
Tarish, Ayoob, 69, 108, 133
Tawila Tanks, 23, *23*
television, 124, *124*
terrace farming, 29, 34, 76
terrorism, 15, 27, 57, 59
thawb (clothing), 116, *116*
Tihamah (coastal plain), 22, 23, 24–
    25, *24*, 32, 80, 104, 110, 111, *118*
tourism, 22, 23, 39, 46, 58, 80, *80*, 105
tower houses, 118–120, *119*
trade, 43, *44*, 75–76
Traditional Heritage House, 105
transportation, 21
Turkish people, 46

U

unification, 11, 54, 55, *55*, 66, 75, 76,
    125–126

United Nations, 40–41, 107
"United Republic" (national anthem), 69, 108, 126
United States, 56, 59, 59, 73, 108
USS *Cole*, 59, 59

V
veiled chameleons, 36, 36
vice presidents, 55, 61, 65, 70
villages. *See also* cities.
    Bedouins in, 86
    Shaharah, 18
volcanoes, 23

W
Wadi Daw'an, 34
Wadi Dhahr, 49
Wadi Hadhramaut, 20, 29, 29, 34, 81
water, 23, 23, 24, 27, 29, 32, 45, 76, 78, 83
water sports, 111
weaving, 104
weddings, 88, 105, 106, 107, 108, 120
wildlife. *See* animal life; insect life; marine life; plant life; reptilian life.
Wisdom of the Yemeni People, The (statue), 13
women. *See also* people.
    child brides, 88
    clothing, 9, 116–117, 117
    education, 88, 88, 90, 123
    employment and, 120
    food and, 114, 114
    Islamic religion and, 92, 94, 94
    literacy rate, 90
    marriage, 88, 88, 120
    Sanaa, 83
    socialization, 123, 123
    Tawakkol Karman, 8, 9–10, 11, 12–13, 14, 15, 17, 46
    Women Journalists Without Chains, 12

Women Journalists Without Chains, 12
World Bank, 27, 82
World War I, 48

Y
Yahya bin Muhammad Hamid al-Din, 48, 49, 49, 50
Yemen Arab Republic (YAR), 11, 51, 54
"Yemen: My Great Nation" (Hajaj Abdulqawi Masaed), 108
Young Pioneers, 54

Z
zakat (Third Pillar of Islam), 98
Zaraniq people, 110, 110
Zayd bin 'Ali, 95, 96
Zaydi sect, 45, 46, 48, 51, 57, 95, 96
Zubayr, Badavi, 107

Meet the Author

LIZ SONNEBORN, A GRADUATE OF SWARTHMORE College, lives in Brooklyn, New York. She has written more than one hundred books for adults and young readers. Sonneborn is the author of numerous volumes for the Enchantment of the World Series, including several on Middle East countries: *Iraq, United Arab Emirates, Kuwait,* and the first edition of *Yemen.*

Working on this second edition, which includes entirely new material, felt both familiar and foreign to Sonneborn. In many ways, Yemen's culture and society have changed little from 2008, when the first edition was published, to 2015, when the second edition was written. But that period was convulsive in terms of Yemen's politics and economy.

"I wanted to explain the various political actors and their shifting allegiances in the simplest way possible," Sonneborn explains. "But just as important, I wanted to convey the experiences of average Yemenis." In addition to reading scholarly books and articles, she kept up on daily news reports of the changing situation. She also consulted social media to understand the mood of the country: "The messages and photos from Yemenis were often heartbreaking, but they also best expressed the emotional toll of the country's recent upheavals."

Photo Credits

Maps by XNR Productions, Inc.